Healing in the Landscape of Prayer

Healing

in the

Landscape

of Prayer

ᆼ

Avery Brooke

MOREHOUSE PUBLISHING
A Continuum imprint
HARRISBURG • LONDON • NEW YORK

Morehouse Publishing, P.O. Box 1321, Harrisburg, PA 17105

Morehouse Publishing, The Tower Building, 11 York Road, London SE1 7NX

Morehouse Publishing is a Continuum imprint.

Earlier versions of chapters 2 and 5 appeared in *Weavings: A Journal of Christian Spiritual Life.* Chapter 7 contains an excerpt reprinted from *Unmasking the Powers* by Walter Fink, © 1986 Fortress Press. Used by permission of Augsburg Fortress. The same chapter contains an excerpt reprinted by permission from *The Demise of the Devil* by Susan R. Garrett, © 1989 Augsburg Fortress.

Cover design: Wesley Hoke

Library of Congress Cataloging-in-Publication Data

Brooke, Avery.
　　Healing in the landscape of prayer / Avery Brooke.
　　　　p. cm.
　　Originally published: Cambridge ; Boston, Mass. : Cowley Publications, c1996.
　　Includes bibliographical references.
　　ISBN 0-8192-2126-0
　　1. Spiritual healing. 2. Prayer—Christianity. I. Title

BT732.5.B76 2004
234'.131—dc22　　　　　　　　　　　　　　　　　　2003068605

Printed in the United States of America

To my past and present colleagues in the healing ministry at Saint Luke's Parish, Darien, Connecticut; to Anne Kimball, who gathered us together; to Bonnie Brown, who taught us; and to Irene Perkins, who became my partner in a wider ministry of healing.

Contents

Acknowledgments

I owe so much to so many that it is impossible to name them all, but I would like to acknowledge the help and support of several general sources and groups.

Thanks are due to many speakers and writers in the healing movement who have led the way and to the clergy and people of Saint Luke's Episcopal Parish for encouraging and supporting a healing ministry among us. I am also grateful to my brothers in Holy Cross Monastery who have nurtured my life of prayer, which is the foundation for everything else I have learned, and who have given me space and quiet to write in a framework of prayer.

Some stories of healing included in this book give the actual names of the person or persons involved. In other accounts names and circumstances have been omitted or changed for privacy, but all the stories are essentially true. I wish to thank those who allowed their stories to be told.

Specific thanks are due to readers of and commentators on part or all of my manuscript: Margaret (Bonnie) Brown, Anne Kimball, Barbara MacMillan, Margaret Anderson, Charlotte Cleghorn, Lynn Runnels, Sonia Ralston, Barbara Edgar, Kim Aycrigg, Francis Tiso, Irene Perkins, and Bede Mudge, OHC.

Without the wonderful institution of inter-library loan this book could not have been written. Requests for nineteenth- and twentieth-century books and articles have been searched out by the Darien Library's superb director of research, Blanche Parker, and summoned to my aid from a wide geographic area.

This would have been a lesser book if it had not been for the perceptive comments of my editors, Cynthia Shattuck and Vicki Black. They made me work much harder than I had planned and they were right! I am grateful.

Last but not least, I wish to thank Jeannie Sandoval, whose untiring patience, encouragement, and help have made the tasks of research and writing much faster and easier than they would have been otherwise.

Preface

There are many books on Christian healing but most of them have been written by unusually gifted and charismatic ministers of healing. I am neither unusually gifted nor—in the popular sense—charismatic. I am a middle-of-the-road Christian who does a lot of praying and who believes that healing should be seen as part of the everyday fabric of Christian life.

Healing is not yet another program designed to entertain many or help a few, but a commitment to join others in restoring a ministry that is central to the gospel. I have written *Healing in the Landscape of Prayer* because I believe healing should be reclaimed to take the central place in the Christian way that it held in the ministry of Jesus and of the early church.

Although this book is primarily intended for the clergy and laity of traditional parish churches with little or no experience of healing, it also includes insights from charismatic Christians that I believe will benefit those of us who worship and study in more traditional parishes and seminaries.

There is a great deal that I haven't said in this brief introduction to the healing ministry. Rather than overwhelm readers with a great deal of unfamiliar material, I have chosen to let people look over my shoulder as I have learned about healing. The way that healing ministry developed and grew in my home parish of Saint Luke's in Darien, Connecticut, will not work for all churches, nor will my own personal experience and point of view be for everyone. But it is my hope that enough of the universal will be found in these particulars to help people, with the aid of the Spirit, to find their own way.

Avery Brooke
Noroton, Connecticut

The Unexpected

W hen we are open to God, we are open to the unexpected. I am seldom as open as I would like to be, but usually open enough to know when God says, "Not this way!", or "How about that?", and I find myself called to walk down an unexpected path. This book tells the story of such an unexpected path, when I found myself called to a healing ministry in my parish of Saint Luke's in Darien, Connecticut.

It was unexpected because I thought my path ahead was settled. It had taken me three years to get my heart, mind, and life into some sort of order after my husband's death. But it was done. I had decided to stay in our old Victorian house and take in house-sharers. The house-sharers helped with chores and were a companionable presence. We became a family. After spending time in prayer in the mornings I wrote, and in the afternoons I saw people for spiritual direction. I congratulated myself on working out a peaceful pattern of life. But my self-congratulations were premature.

The unexpected began simply enough. In our parish we have a quiet day during Lent. It usually lasts from 9 a.m. to 4 p.m. on a Saturday. A speaker makes several addresses and the rest of the day is left for silent prayer and meditation. One year the publicity announced that Franklin (Skip) Vilas, an Episcopal priest, would speak to us on spiritual healing. The day would end with a service of healing and the laying on of hands.

I had no trouble believing in the reality of spiritual healing. As a spiritual director I had seen many miracles of
spiritual and psychological growth as I watched the action
of God within the people with whom I was privileged to
work. I had also read of many carefully documented modern physical healings, similar to those done by Jesus and
his disciples. There seemed to be few of them in our times,
but too many, I believed, to simply explain away. But I had
never felt called to further involvement with spiritual healing. My life was full and I was content. I came to the quiet
day, therefore, with only mild interest, spiced with a dash
of Lenten obligation.

I remember little of what was said on that Saturday
eight years ago. Nor were there, to my knowledge, any no-
table healings. But when Skip Vilas invited people to come
forward, one by one, for the laying on of hands, he also
said that friends and others who were moved to join him
and lay hands on the shoulders or back of the person he
was praying for should feel free to do so. When it was my
turn for prayer, I was therefore not surprised to feel several
hands on my back at the altar rail, but I was startled to
feel that one pair of hands was hot. I don't mean just
warm, but *hot*—like a radiator. I was distracted from Skip's
prayer for me. I vaguely remembered that hot hands were
associated with healing. Whose hands were they? When
the prayer was over, I turned around quickly and found
that the hands belonged to Margaret, a woman who had
been coming to me for spiritual direction.

Now one of the tasks of a spiritual director is spiritual
discernment. We are supposed to be wise about prayer and
open to God so that we can discern the motions of the
Spirit within our directees. Margaret had been coming to
me for two years, and I had had no idea that she had what

I now perceived must be a gift of healing. I felt shocked and abashed.

A week or so after the quiet day, Anne Kimball, our associate rector, contacted Bonnie Brown, a Congregational minister with a vocation to the ministry of healing, and asked if she would be willing to teach a group at Saint Luke's something about healing. Bonnie told Anne that she would be happy to do so, that in fact she would very much like the experience of teaching a group of people in a liturgical church something about spiritual healing. When I heard of the group I felt that I should join.

The twelve people that Anne Kimball gathered together were all women, most of us at retirement age. No one held a full-time job, and so we were able to gather every other Tuesday afternoon under Bonnie Brown's tutelage. Bonnie is an unusual and remarkably gifted person, not only as a minister of healing but also as a teacher and therapist. She lost her faith while in seminary and chose not to be ordained. She regained it about twenty years ago through an unexpected combination of New Age meditation and Roman Catholic charismatic healing—God's unexpected action again!

Bonnie had polio as a child and is in a wheelchair. She went to the late Agnes Sanford (one of the great ministers of healing) for prayer when she was sixteen. No cure resulted, but it seems probable to me that Bonnie's innate gift of healing was enhanced through Agnes Sanford's prayer. People who are gifted in healing often do not discover it until they are older, but Bonnie remembers being known in college for the "magic back rubs" she could give her classmates.

We in the group at Saint Luke's thought of ourselves as broad-minded; certainly we felt that we were one with Christians of other denominations. But as Bonnie began to teach us, we discovered difficulties in communication. She spoke "Congregationalese," and we were strong Episcopalians. We had also thought we were broad-minded about Roman Catholic charismatic healing and New Age meditation. But they, too, have different languages. In addition to these difficulties, we had a certain timidity in learning about healing. It was intriguing, yes, but also a bit frightening. However, as time went on, these problems seemed to melt away. Difficulties in communication vanished, and we realized that Bonnie was a rather awesome and very humble Christian. She led us—ever so gently—through prayer and meditation to the laying on of hands and specific, unrehearsed healing prayers for one another.

I think that we had all come to the group with a more distant and intellectual vision of learning about healing. Although we did read books, what we learned were primarily interior and spiritual lessons acquired through practice and through Bonnie's guiding words. I remember her voice time and again saying, "Get your egos out of the way. Make room for God." We weren't even quite sure what she meant at first, but as I have learned over the years, this dynamic is at the crux of healing. It is not *our* compassion that heals, it is *God's* compassion. It is not our words of prayer that heal, it is God using our words and our hands and the energy flowing through us.

We soon found that our own hands would sometimes get as hot as radiators. Later we learned that heat and the feeling of energy flowing through our hands were not necessary for God to bring healing. Even words were not necessary, and wordless prayer was often best. But, silently or aloud, we have always held to Jesus' command to his disciples to go out and heal in his name.

These aspects of healing were not clear to us for many, many months. We only knew that *something* was happening within and among us. We were too shy to talk about it, but we knew the Holy Spirit was with us. We learned—ever so slowly—not to *worry* about the words of our prayers and to let the Spirit choose our words for us. We struggled to get our egos, ourselves, out of the way.

In a larger sense, the whole ministry of the church is healing. Working for peace and justice is healing, serving in a soup kitchen is healing, volunteering in a hospital, working with troubled youth—are all healing ministries. But the more specific ministry of healing that Bonnie was teaching us is not something *we* do, it is something *God* does. We just get ourselves out of the way, as best we can, to let God through.

Some of us didn't talk to anyone about what we were doing in the group. Would people think we were setting ourselves up as "holier than thou" if they knew we were laying on hands and praying for healing? We shuddered. We did not like to think of ourselves as "channels for God." It seemed presumptuous. It was more comfortable to be humble. But was it humility to refuse to do what Jesus told his disciples to do? The Bible is very clear on the subject:

> Jesus called the twelve together and gave them power and authority over all demons and to cure diseases, and he sent them out to proclaim the kingdom of God and to heal. (Luke 9:1-2)

In the Acts of the Apostles, Jesus' followers did just as they were told by the Lord to do. Probably the most familiar story of healing in Acts is of Peter and John healing the man who had been lame from birth (Acts 3:1-16). My favorite story about Paul and healing is told in Acts 14, where he and Barnabas were proclaimed gods by the people of Lystra because of a miraculous healing. Protesting, they tore their clothes and rushed out into the crowd, shouting, "Friends, why are you doing this? We are mortals just like you."

Another familiar text we studied concerning healing in the New Testament is from James:

> Are any among you sick? They should call for the elders of the church and have them pray over them, anointing them with oil in the name of the Lord. The power of faith will save the sick, and the Lord will raise them up. (James 5:14-15)

We began to think more about *obedience* than seeming humble. Wanting to "seem humble," after all, was an inverse kind of pride. It was also ego getting in the way of God.

Perhaps because I had been professionally involved in talking about God in my writing and during my years in religious publishing, I found little difficulty in talking about my involvement in healing. And once I spoke up, I began to hear other people's stories of healing.

One was from an elderly but lively woman who seemed to radiate a health and happiness I noted as soon as I met her. She looked very much at peace with herself and her world and a sparkle of humor showed in her eyes. After I had mentioned my interest in healing, she took me aside and said she would like to tell me her story.

"Soon after the birth of my first child," she said, "my daughter was diagnosed with a serious disease. It was incurable, the doctors told us, and she would probably die soon. My husband and I were stunned. One weekday, when the baby and I were alone, I wrapped her up warmly—it was winter—and I drove to our church. I carried her into the church and walked right up to the altar rail. I knelt down there with the baby in my arms and prayed. Suddenly I felt a great force streaming through my body into the child's. When it faded," she concluded, "I realized that the baby was well."

"What did you do then?" I asked.

"I took her to the doctor, who confirmed that she was completely cured, and then I went to see my rector. He told me to tell no one, but to go and see one of the sisters he knew at the nearby convent. She became my spiritual director, and I've been going to the convent all these years. Until recently, I have told no one. But lately it has seemed right to break the silence. My daughter is now an adult and is married with a child of her own."

While on retreat I met an Episcopal priest who told me that he had had a late vocation to the priesthood. He was married and had children, and his seminary years were a difficult time for him and his family. Toward the end of his preparation for the priesthood, he developed a very bad sacroiliac and had been in quite a bit of pain. Now one leg was completely numb.

"I know it doesn't make sense," he said, "but I was terribly concerned that *nothing* stand in the way of my becoming a priest after all I'd put my family through. I thought if I went to the doctor about my back and leg, someone might say, 'Sorry, but you can't be a priest if you're crippled,' so I didn't go to a doctor and I arrived at my first job without having sought medical help.

"It just so happened," he continued, "that my first job was at Saint Boniface Church in Sarasota, Florida, where a special kind of healing ministry had been instituted. I called to make an appointment. I didn't tell them anything about my back, but just said that since I was new at Saint Boniface, I felt I should learn about their work. When the time came, I entered the room where two people trained in healing were waiting for me. I sat down and we said the Lord's Prayer together. We prayed for quite a while in silence. Suddenly I felt one of the healing minister's hands slip in between the chair and my back and rest on the small of my back. All was still again. Time passed and then, without warning, there was a loud crack! Suddenly, all pain and numbness were gone. I sat up and said, 'My God. It worked!' And the three of us dissolved into laughter."

☙

During the time I was hearing these stories, back at Saint Luke's nothing dramatic was happening, though I was comforted by the fact that healing ministers at Saint Boniface trained for four years. Looking back on those early years, we can now see that small physical, psychological, and spiritual healings *were* occurring. But bad backs, mild depression, and various aches and pains come and go, and it was less frightening for us to think that something other than prayer was responsible for those healings. We could give God credit if it was a new pill or treatment, but we weren't ready to say that *our* prayers and *our* laying on of hands in Jesus' name had anything to do with it. We preferred to think that our words were helpful because they were comforting and our presence and concern were strengthening because they made people feel less alone, rather than to admit that *God* might actually be using us to heal in some way we didn't understand. And yet, we knew that *something* was happening to us and through us when we met.

Animals, I learned from reading, are very open to healing, as they have none of our rational defenses. When my husband died he left behind a young standard poodle named Ceildh (pronounced Kaylee). *Ceildh* is a Celtic word for the ancient custom of gathering together at a neighbor's house to tell stories and sing songs. We had just returned from a trip to the Outer Hebrides and the word *ceildh* was on our minds. But now my husband was gone and I left the house early for a long day in the city. Ceildh was lonely, and while I was gone he adopted the dog and family across the street. My neighbors were remarkably accepting of this at first, but when Ceildh not only chased cars but began teaching their dog to chase cars, they said, "I'm sorry, but *something will have to be done*."

My best friends lived on the other side of town and liked dogs, so I appealed to them and they took Ceildh in. This way Ceildh would not be lonely and I could at least see him, on my frequent visits. I was very fond of Ceildh.

Some years passed and one day my friend called up. "I'm afraid I have bad news. I took Ceildh to the vet for his annual shots and he had a severe reaction. The vet said, 'Once in a great while this happens. We've done everything we can. I'm terribly sorry. You brought me a healthy dog and now Ceildh is dying. He'll be more comfortable at home so why don't you take him with you. Bring him back at the end of the week and we'll give him a shot to put him to sleep.'

"I'm going to be out, but if you want to see Ceildh," my friend continued, "I'll leave the back door open."

So late that day I went over and found Ceildh all alone in the living room. I looked down at him sadly and he lifted his tail briefly and then let it fall.

Standing there I suddenly realized that I could do more than give him a hug. Why not? He was God's creature, too. I knelt down, put my arms around him and said out loud, "Ceildh, in the name of the Lord Jesus Christ, I ask that you be restored to full health." I left my hands there for a few moments, prayed without words, and then said, "Amen." I patted him gently and left.

The next morning my friend called and said, "Ceildh seems a bit better." Well, I thought, I'd better go back and pray some more. I did, and again Ceildh improved. I went again on the third day. By the fourth day Ceildh was well. "A miracle," said the vet.

Was it a miracle? Well, in any case it was an unexplained physical healing. I just thanked God for the healing and left it at that. Only God knew the why of it.

Not only are animals less resistant to healing prayers than human beings, often their healing persuades a reluctant Christian to follow a call into the healing ministry. Susan, who later joined our group at Saint Luke's, first realized the power of healing prayer when she prayed for a badly crippled dog who got well. Another woman, who has been a minister of healing for many years, told me that she did not realize she had a gift of healing until she was forty-five, when a puppy who had been run over by a car was brought to her for prayer. The puppy was obviously dying, badly crushed and in pain. An hour after she prayed, the dog was happily running around the house.

∾

In spite of being uncertain that healings were actually happening in our small group, I found myself experiencing an inner push to lay on hands and pray for people outside the group as well. I can only describe this inner push as a movement of the Spirit. I would find myself saying—in a very light tone—to someone in distress at a party, in a museum, or visiting my home, "Would you like a little spiritual healing?" Usually they would be surprised, but say, "Yes," and I would then lay on hands and pray (silently and unobtrusively if we were in public).

I have an old school friend who is a painter. We meet at least once a year in the Metropolitan Museum to look at some paintings, have lunch, and then look at more paintings. Miriam is a Conservative Jew whose spiritual leanings have grown stronger over the years, and since we have known each other well for a long time, we can talk easily about spiritual matters as well as anything else in our lives.

Over lunch on this particular day, I spoke to her of my growing involvement with healing, and she told me that the doctor had said she was going blind. As we returned to the galleries after lunch, I felt that inner push to lay on hands, fueled not only by the Spirit, but by my love and compassion for my old friend. It kept haunting me as we walked through the galleries and distracted me from the paintings. Finally I said, "Miriam, I would very much like to lay on hands and pray for your eyes. How would you feel about that?"

"Fine," she answered.

We found a quiet corner in the Japanese meditation room. Putting a hand on her shoulder, I silently prayed that Miriam's eyes would be healed. The prayer was quite brief and then I said, "Amen," softly but audibly. Miriam looked up and said, "I feel the most incredible sense of peace." It is now five years later, and she has not gone blind. Is it because of that prayer? A mistaken diagnosis? A change in medicine? Only God knows.

Although caught up by now in more and more aspects of healing, a part of me fought it. What was happening to that simple life of writing in the morning and seeing directees in the afternoon? It was still the basic structure of my life, but my schedule kept getting interrupted. I complained to Bede, the monk who was my spiritual director, "I don't have time for this!"

"And just how," he responded, "do you think God calls us to do something?"

"Oh," I said. And from then on, I relaxed into it and, as best I could, let God take the lead.

Bonnie Brown was still teaching us at this point. Anne Kimball was our clergy liaison at Saint Luke's and faithfully supported the group until her resignation in early 1994 to become assistant dean of Berkeley Divinity School. But I realized that sooner or later we would need a lay head of the group. "Anne," I said one day, "I don't know whether a lay head gets appointed or elected, but I've finally stopped arguing with God about spending time on healing. I'd like to offer myself for the job."

"You're appointed," she said. "You've really been leading us for some time, you know!" she added with a smile.

❧

It was two years from the time of our first meeting with Bonnie before the group at Saint Luke's realized that we wanted to offer to the whole parish the praying we had learned to do for each other. It took another year of prayer and planning before we were ready to hold services of healing.

Now that our ministry was becoming more public, we were faced with a number of theological questions with practical implications: Who has "a gift of healing" and how does he or she receive it? Obviously gifts came from God, but how? Were people born with gifts? Did they only develop with a born-again visitation of the Holy Spirit? I knew that I personally did not have a special gift of healing, nor did most of our group. A few—like Margaret, the directee whose hot hands I had experienced at the quiet day—had somewhat more of a gift than most of us, but no one seemed to have those startling gifts we read about in the lives of great ministers of healing. Many of our hands—including my own—now often became "hot as a radiator" and we could sometimes feel a rush of energy coming through us, as could the one we were praying for. But we still did not feel we had a special gift.

One way of looking at gifts helped my understanding. I asked a woman with a very obvious gift of healing to help me in my confusion. "It's simple," she said. "It's like playing the piano. Everyone can learn to play the piano. Some never learn to play well, others learn very well. And some have a gift."

Her explanation rang true to me. Having a gift was not an all-or-nothing affair. Jesus told *all* his disciples to "go and heal," not some. *All* Christians have a gift of healing by virtue of baptism, though some of us practice using that gift more than others.

What then of the gifts of the Spirit which came to the disciples at Pentecost and are the foundation of Pentecostal beliefs today? From the New Testament it is clear that early Christians believed not only in baptism but in a second "baptism of the Spirit." In some denominations today this has been incorporated into the rite of confirmation. Undoubtedly the Holy Spirit does come during confirmation, but it is usually a quiet coming. Few confirmands find themselves suddenly filled with holy joy and speaking in tongues.

Most Pentecostalists and charismatics believe that this more intense experience of the Spirit is necessary for a person to be able to have and minister healing gifts. At Saint Luke's we found that was not necessarily true. The Spirit had come to us quietly not only in our baptisms and confirmations, but as we prayed for each other's healing. The Spirit is the ultimate Teacher of prayer and more and more we knew the Spirit was within us, teaching, guiding, and healing. We were not against the more intense experience, but we also knew that if we sought it and openly spoke in tongues most people in our traditional parish would have nothing to do with healing.

○ℬ

By and large our healing ministry for people at Saint Luke's has remained one of small and quiet inner miracles. But occasionally we are surprised. Recently, Bobbie, one of our members, was assisting in a course we were giving. After a presentation we broke into small groups to pray for one another. Bobbie had a mole below one eye that had grown so high it was interfering with her sight. She had a date for surgery the next day to have it removed and she asked for and received prayers that the surgery would go well. The next morning she looked in the mirror and there was no mole to be seen. The doctor couldn't understand it.

At an earlier time Bobbie herself was praying at a service for a man with a kidney stone that was to be operated on the next day. When she prayed, the man felt sure that something had happened. He asked for another X-ray. The doctor said that there was no possibility that the stone could have passed unnoticed and an X-ray was not needed. The man insisted. The kidney stone was gone.

On another occasion, a woman came to our group with severe endometriosis. We prayed for her several times. One day I suggested we try a longer time. She agreed and we had her lie on a sofa for fifteen minutes of mostly silent prayer. When the time was up she didn't move. We stayed near and let her remain. After about ten minutes she opened her eyes and said that the pain was all gone. "It's the first time the pain has been gone in five years," she said. "And I felt closer to God than I ever have in my life."

One Easter Sunday I looked up at the altar and suddenly realized that I had a blind spot in one eye. I looked down at my prayer book, closed my other eye, and saw that indeed there was a spot in my eye where the type got all fuzzy. I couldn't read with that eye. My eye doctor said that I had a full thickness macula hole. My macula, which is the central part of the retina and the part with which the eye focuses, had dropped out. With the good eye closed I could not read either books or street signs. Since the good eye compensated most of the time, it wasn't too bad—but it might happen in the good eye, too. I had to go every three months to check.

Six months later the doctor said, "Hmph, it's improving."

In nine months my eye had gone from 20/400 vision to 20/30 vision.

"What are the chances of this happening?" I asked.

"In my experience there are none," he replied. "I've seen improvement before, but never to this degree."

"Well," I suggested, "maybe I'm learning to use peripheral cells to focus."

"Peripheral cells do not give this level of vision," he replied. "Besides, it's regenerated."

"Well," I said hesitantly, "I've been involved in spiritual healing."

"Hmph," he said.

But as my eye continued to regenerate he softened and we began to talk. Later a nun came in with macular degeneration. Her sisters prayed and *she* began to improve. On my last visit he told me of another patient. "She has," he said, "the same problem you had. I told her there was nothing I could do for her. Then I told her your story and suggested that if her church had a prayer group she should ask for prayers."

On the day my doctor told me that my eye had regenerated, I hurried home to look at my calendar. Along with others from our healing group, I had been going to healing conferences in various parts of the country. I wanted to relate the date when he first noted improvement to whatever conference I'd been to around that time. Some gifted healer, I thought, had been a channel for God's healing grace for me. I looked at my calendar and found that I hadn't *been* to a conference in the three months in which the healing had started. The only people who had prayed for me were the ordinary Saint Luke's parishioners in our healing group.

Christian Healing through the Ages

In the spring of 1990 I began to learn something about the history of Christian healing because I was asked to write an article about it for *Weavings*, an ecumenical journal of spirituality. Writing about something is the best way for me to learn, and learning was what I wanted to do.

The impact that my research into healing made on me was very deep; what I could discover about the history of healing seemed at the same time to connect with the stories of healing in the Bible and with those I knew of first-hand. However simple our experiences, they were cut from the same piece of cloth. I found myself telling the stories I learned to our group at Saint Luke's with as much excitement as I would if they had happened yesterday to a friend of mine, because the stories were so clearly connected with the healings I was experiencing in my own life and in the group at Saint Luke's.

However, the history of healing, I soon found, was not easy to explore. It was clear enough in the Bible: so much of Jesus' ministry was a ministry of healing that if you took a copy of the gospels and cut out all mention of healing or the casting out of demons, all you would have left would be paper lace. This emphasis on healing also permeates the book of Acts, yet I found it difficult to find any mention of healing whatsoever in modern histories of the post-biblical church. I could not believe that what was clearly a part of the Christian way for the early disciples would disappear so completely in the years immediately following. And yet when I took down from my shelves the first volumes of two three-volume histories of the church, I could find no mention of healing. Further work in the library still yielded nothing. Eventually I was rescued from frustration by Morton Kelsey's original version of a book called *Healing and Christianity*,[1] which opened doors of understanding for me and led the way to other sources.

The reason I could not find anything about Christian healing in my church history books became increasingly apparent to me. The continuing influence of the scientific rationalism of both the Renaissance and Enlightenment on scholars of our own century is one of those realities that is so basic and all-pervasive in our culture that we sometimes forget it is there. For centuries, education has been based on a rational understanding of life. As we know, this has been positive in many ways, but it has also had the negative effect of minimizing or even denigrating the life of the spirit. Consequently, Christian healing has never been considered academically respectable. When seeking to uncover the history of healing in the church, Morton Kelsey and a handful of other writers in our own day had to go back to the original source material to uncover the existence of healing in the early church.

In the second and third centuries, healing, far from being nonexistent, was taken for granted as part of the Christian way. Justin Martyr, a second-century Greek philosopher and convert, argued Christianity's case to the Roman senate and the emperor, Marcus Aurelius, by pointing out that Christians, in the name of Jesus Christ, drove out demons and healed people when no one else could do so. Irenaeus, one

---

1. Morton T. Kelsey, *Healing and Christianity: A Classic Study*, rev. ed. (Minneapolis: Augsburg/Fortress, 1994).

of the most brilliant Christian apologists, wrote of an en-
tire church that devoted itself to prayer and fasting "and
so brought someone back from death," while Tertullian, a
lay theologian born thirty years later, wrote in his treatise
On the Resurrection of the Flesh, "God, whom you have discovered to be the restorer of all things, is likewise the re-
viver of the flesh."

Early in the fourth century, the emperor Constantine
granted freedom of worship to his subjects and Christianity gained a new and favored status. The impact of this on
the church was vast and had many repercussions on both
religious and political life. It was no longer the church of
the martyrs, and without the threat of martyrdom it became much easier to become a Christian. As the churches
were flooded with casual Christians, healing became less
frequent. Some Christians attempting to keep alive the
spirit of martyrdom and self-sacrifice drew apart to live a
life of prayer in the deserts of Syria and Egypt.

Typical of these Christians who fled to the desert was
Basil of Caesarea, who was educated in Cappadocia, Caesarea, Constantinople, and Athens in some of the best
Greek and Christian facilities of the time. In 358 he
moved to the desert, where he met his old friend Gregory
of Nazianzus; together they went on preaching missions
until Basil was appointed Bishop of Caesarea in 370.

Basil founded and maintained a public hospital outside
Caesarea. In his writings he wondered—in a way we would
consider modern—whether turning to medicine was in
keeping with religious piety. He concluded that medical
science had been given to us by God, and that to reject en-
tirely the benefits to be derived was "the sign of a petty
nature." Basil's beliefs helped to lay the foundation for
centuries of Christian commitment to caring for the sick
and building hospitals for them as well as praying for heal-

ing, although the connection between spiritual and medical healing has been neglected in later centuries.

Basil's brother and sister, Gregory of Nyssa and Macrina, were also influential leaders of the church at the time: like Basil, Gregory became a bishop and theologian, while Macrina founded a monastery for men and women on the family estate in Cappadocia. Gregory was so impressed by Macrina's life that he decided to write her biography.

A Roman officer who heard Gregory wanted anecdotes for the biography came forward and told the story of his visit to Macrina's community some years earlier, along with his wife and daughter. Upon arrival, the officer went to the men's quarters while his wife and little girl visited Macrina in the women's quarters. The child had a badly infected eye, and the eyeball was swollen and white. Macrina took the child in her arms and kissed the eye.

"Do me a favor," Macrina said, "and stay for dinner. In return, I'll give you some medicine for the child's eye."

So they stayed for dinner and then went on their way home. During the journey the wife suddenly remembered that she'd forgotten the medicine. In consternation she turned toward their child and then exclaimed to her husband, "Look! We don't need any other medicine! Macrina gave us the cure that comes from prayer and it's already worked!" There was no sign left of the disease.[2]

The theological writings of Basil of Caesarea, Gregory of Nyssa, and Gregory of Nazianzus—who became known as the Cappadocian Fathers—are filled with references to healing. They lived during the time that the definitions of Christian faith were being hammered out, and they partici-

---

2. See Saint Gregory of Nyssa, *The Life of St. Macrina*, in his *Ascetical Works*, trans. Virginia Woods Callahan, vol. 58 of *The Fathers of the Church: A New Translation* (Washington, D.C.: The Catholic University Press, 1967), pp. 188-190 (my paraphrase).

pated and were influential in these debates. Particularly in the writings of Gregory of Nyssa, it is apparent that belief in God's power to heal influenced his theology. This is not surprising, since those basic questions about the relationship of spirit and matter, body and soul, in Christ Jesus are reflected in both physical and spiritual healing.

It is certainly partly due to the teaching of these desert fathers that the Eastern Orthodox churches have an unbroken history of healing.

⊙

Healing became associated with the liturgy of the church quite early, not only in the eucharist, but also in the baptismal rite. Cyprian, bishop of Carthage and a martyr of the church, wrote in the third century that baptism itself was "sometimes the means by which a serious illness was cured." The eucharist is a healing and redemptive liturgy in a larger sense, but it was also viewed at that time as a specific agent of healing. Oil, later reserved for anointing the sick, was offered up with the bread and wine in the eucharist. The oil could then be used in church, brought by a priest when visiting the sick, or taken home by lay Christians for anointing sick family members.

In due course, special services of healing were developed with the laying on of hands and anointing with oil. These liturgies could become quite elaborate, with several priests and lay people visiting the sick person at home. They began by exorcising and blessing the house. Then the sick person knelt for the laying on of hands and was anointed on the throat, breast, and back, and more liberally anointed where the pain was greatest. Prayers of thanksgiving were made, the patient was told to pray for recovery and to make a confession of sin. The eucharist then followed. This group of priests and lay people—or part of it—came back every week until the person was well.

○ヾ

By the time of Saint Augustine, whose lifetime spanned the fourth and fifth centuries, we find fewer accounts of miraculous healings. In his early writings Augustine stated that Christians should not expect to exercise the powers of healing as they had at the time of Jesus and the apostles, but later he changed his mind. Three years before his death, when revising his great work, *The City of God*, Augustine corrected his earlier statement and said that although healings were rare, they still occurred. The reason for this change of heart was a personal experience of healing, which he relates in *The City of God*.

A shrine containing the relics of Saint Stephen had been erected in Augustine's church in Hippo. Two weeks before Easter in the year 424, a brother and sister began to come each day to pray for healing at the shrine. Both suffered from constant convulsive seizures. On Easter morning, Augustine was waiting in the vestibule for the procession to start, and the boy was praying by the shrine. Suddenly, Augustine was aware of a disturbance in the church: the boy had fallen to the floor and a moment later had risen up, completely cured.

Augustine invited the boy back to Easter dinner, and they talked. In the following days, Augustine preached about the martyrs and healing. On the third day after Easter, Augustine read the young man's statement while the boy and girl stood on the choir steps where they could be seen—the boy cured, but the girl still convulsed. Augustine thanked them and the boy went back to his place, but his sister went to the shrine to pray. Suddenly, she too fell down and rose up healed. The church broke into a joyful pandemonium.

Nevertheless, by the fifth century the practice of healing was no longer part of a common ministry in the church, but was the exception to the rule. It is interesting to compare the lives of two fourth-century monks to see the beginning of a change in attitudes toward healing. The biography of Saint Martin of Tours, who brought monasticism from the desert to France, lists one healing after another. In one account Saint Martin returns to the monastery after a trip to find that a young monk has died. Martin weeps, and then,

> laying hold, as it were, of the Holy Spirit, with the whole powers of his mind, he ordered the others to quit the cell in which the body was lying; and bolting the door, he stretched himself at full length on the dead limbs of the departed brother. Having given himself for some time to earnest prayer, and perceiving by means of the Spirit of God that power was present, he then rose up for a little, and gazing on the countenance of the deceased, he waited without misgiving for the result of his prayer and of the mercy of the Lord. And scarcely had the space of two hours elapsed when he saw the dead man begin to move a little in all his members, and to tremble with his eyes opened.[3]

On the other hand, John Cassian—whose *Conferences* were specified by Saint Benedict to be read aloud every day to the monks—had a largely negative assessment of healing. He believed that miraculous healings occurred, but claimed that miracles were performed to demonstrate the power of the Lord to heretics or scoffers, or else be-

---

3. Sulpitius Severus, *Life of St. Martin*, 7, in vol. 2 of *The Nicene and Post-Nicene Fathers* (Grand Rapids: Eerdmans, 1956), p. 7.

cause a monk was pestered for healing. Exhibiting none of the compassion of Martin of Tours, Cassian saw healing as a way for monks to lose their humility rather than as a way for the sick to get well, and he warned that it was spiritually dangerous to involve oneself in the ministry of healing.

By the time of Pope Gregory the Great in the late sixth and early seventh centuries, a major change was occurring in attitudes toward sickness and health. At a time of breakup and turbulence when civilization was seen as falling apart, Gregory and eventually all Christians came to regard sickness as a discipline sent from God. This change in understanding was a complete reversal of the earlier belief that God sent health and healing power, not illness.

As large cities fell into ruin, small towns were deserted, and one catastrophe followed another, people no longer expected a happy and healthy life; the most they hoped for was Paradise. Unction for healing became unction for dying—the last rites. A healing element persisted in the practice, in that anointing healed people of their sins, but the purpose was to speed them to Paradise, not to bring them healing in this world. Only priests could give last rites, and the ministry of healing for physical and mental illness was largely forgotten by the ninth and tenth centuries.

Monasteries had long been places where the sick were cared for, but a church council in 1139 declared that monks could not study medicine, and in 1163 churchmen were prohibited from performing surgery. However, if a doctor visiting a sick person did not first summon a priest, the doctor would be excommunicated. When the priest came, the end of the visit was signaled when a hairshirt was placed on the floor. The patient was laid upon it, signed with a cross of ashes, and asked whether ashes and haircloth were pleasing as evidence of his or her penitence.

The patient was to answer, "Yes, they are pleasing," and then the priest would leave.

This attitude toward illness and spiritual healing has lingered until very recently. The English *Book of Common Prayer* contains the following exhortation for use when visiting the sick: "Whatsoever your sickness is, know you certainly that it is God's visitation." It further suggests that you should "render humble thanks" for that sickness. Out of curiosity, I took my mother's wedding prayer book off the shelf. It was the 1908 version of the American *Book of Common Prayer*, and there were the same prayers. They were in slightly modernized language, but no less stark.

∞

After Gregory, Christian healing did continue in some form, although it was not part of the liturgy or of common Christian practice. It continued through the healing miracles of saints and through the relics of saints and martyrs, and neither means of healing has ever been repudiated by the Roman Catholic Church. Indeed, miracles, usually of healing, became part of the necessary proof of sanctity before a saint could be canonized. Often these miracles occurred after a saint's death.

This phenomenon of miracles after death started with the martyrs. In the fourth century, John Chrysostom wrote, "The bodies of the martyrs have been left on earth so that Christians may reach out to them for healing."[4] And Christians did. Here we have a foreshadowing of all the relics and pilgrimages that became so much a part of the piety of the Middle Ages, but in the early church the

---

4. Saint John Chrysostom, *Baptismal Instructions*, 7.5, in vol. 31 of *Ancient Christian Writers* (Westminster, Md.: The Newman Press, 1963), pp. 105-106.

martyrs were a fresher memory. There is, for instance, the shrine of the forty martyrs of Sebaste, a town in Armenia, where forty soldiers were denounced as Christians. They were forced to stand naked on the ice of a frozen pond with baths of hot water on the banks tempting them to give way and deny Christ. Only one did, and his place was immediately taken by a heretofore unbelieving soldier. All forty froze to death.

Their bodies were burned and later a shrine was built, where soldiers brought their sick and wounded and often spent the night. This practice was called "incubation." Gregory of Nyssa tells of a lame soldier who spent the night there. In a dream, the soldier heard a voice: "Lame one, give me your foot that I may touch it." The soldier dreamed of pulling his leg forward. There was a wrenching noise—loud enough to wake both him and his companions—and he stood up, cured.[5]

As time went on, relics of martyrs and saints became much sought after. Pilgrimages to see or touch the relics became tremendously popular and were made by both the ill and the well. Thousands of miracles were claimed, and hagiography—the art of writing the lives of the saints—became an exercise in fanciful imagination. In the Roman Catholic Church, with its heavy reliance on the theology of Aquinas and his well-reasoned exposition of the Christian faith, healing remained largely in the domain of saints and their relics both during and after the Reformation.

∝

5. Morton T. Kelsey, *Healing and Christianity*, p. 136. See also *The Oxford Dictionary of the Christian Church*, ed. F. L. Cross (London: Oxford University Press, 1957), p. 1235.

By the time of the Reformation healing shrines had become commercial ventures, so it was no wonder that Luther and Calvin rejected healing along with other practices that had become corrupt. Yet at the heart of the Reformation was the authority of the Bible—and there in the Bible were all of Jesus' healings and those of his disciples. Scripture brought the reformers face-to-face with healing. Luther argued that the healings recorded in Scripture took place only to get the church started, and that the "greater works than these" that Jesus promised the disciples they would perform in his name were *spiritual* works, the saving of souls. Like Augustine, Luther's attitude toward healing softened in his last years. He prayed for his friend Melancthon when he was ill, who recovered, and later he wrote a service of healing. Many of his followers, however, stayed with his earlier views.

Healing continued among other Protestant churches, but it was met with open criticism. For instance, George Fox, founder of the Society of Friends in the seventeenth century, wrote a *Book of Miracles* recounting one hundred fifty healings, but the manuscript was later destroyed by his followers, who feared its effect on their critics.[6] Some British and American Baptists in the early seventeenth century also practiced healing and endured severe criticism. John Wesley, Anglican priest and founder of Methodism, also wrote of healing through prayer. Once, he records, on the way to an important preaching mission, his horse went lame. Putting his hand on the horse, he prayed, and the horse was cured. It was as simple as that. Other Protestant groups, including Mennonites and Moravians, also practiced praying for the sick.

---

6. This manuscript has been partially reconstructed from other sources: Henry J. Cadbury, *George Fox's Book of Miracles* (London: Cambridge University Press, 1948). It contains extensive scholarly commentary.

⊗

In the nineteenth century we see the first stirrings of a true revival in the ministry of healing. The Roman Catholic Church witnessed a great resurgence of interest in pilgrimage to healing shrines, the most famous of which is Lourdes. During this time miracles of healing at shrines and in the lives of modern saints began to be documented more carefully.

In 1842, in a village at the edge of the Black Forest, a Lutheran pastor named Johann Blumhardt prayed for a parishioner whom the New Testament writers would have described as possessed by demons and we in our day as mentally ill. After a long spiritual battle, she got well, and people began to flock to his church for prayer and healing. The Lutheran authorities were alarmed and in 1846 forbade him to include prayers for physical healing. He replied that it was impossible for him to be the pastor and not to have healings simply happen. The authorities were persuaded—after long argument—and he was allowed to continue. The sick flocked to his church and in 1852 he opened a "faith home," or house of healing, in Bad Boll, which soon became famous and had a vast influence.

Dorothea Trudel, a young Swiss florist and devout Protestant whose mother had brought her up to believe in the healing power of Jesus, also became known for her ministry of healing. She prayed and anointed her sick colleagues with oil and they were instantaneously healed. As a result, people in need of healing beat a path to her door. Eventually, she was brought to trial for practicing medicine without a license; when she won her case, the resulting publicity brought even more people. To accommodate them, Trudel opened several homes for healing.

The late nineteenth-century revival of healing in America started simply enough. In 1846 a man called Ethan D. Allen was healed of tuberculosis after Methodist class leaders prayed for him. Allen immediately began a full-time ministry of healing. Poorly educated and very shy, he never spoke to large audiences but concentrated on healing the poor in churches, homes, and poorhouses throughout the eastern United States for fifty years, gathering many disciples as he traveled. One of his disciples, Elizabeth Mix, a better educated and more articulate speaker than Allen, became the first African-American healing evangelist in America.

Ethan Allen was influenced by the Holiness revival within the Methodist Church; the name arose from John Wesley's doctrine that complete holiness, or perfect sanctification, was attainable and should be the goal of all Christians. Many in the Holiness movement began to teach that such holiness could be reached instantaneously through the baptism of the Spirit. This departure from Wesley's idea of gradual sanctification led to their split from Methodism and eventually to the founding of Pentecostalism.

The Holiness revival reached beyond Methodism. One convert was Dr. Charles Cullis, a life-long Episcopalian and homeopathic physician from Boston. Grief-stricken by the death of his young wife, Cullis attended a Holiness meeting in New York City and experienced a deep conversion that led him to vow to minister to the sick, the poor, and the hopeless for the rest of his life. His healing ministry served to convince many American Protestants of the validity of Christian healing.

With his great intelligence and organizational abilities, Cullis established four homes where tuberculosis patients who would have been summarily dismissed from hospitals because they were unable to pay could die in dignity. He started similar homes for people who were paralyzed, insane, or suffering from spinal injuries or cancer.

In 1869 Cullis read a life of Dorothea Trudel and visited her houses of healing in Switzerland, along with those of Johann Blumhardt. Inspired by their examples, he healed a woman of a brain tumor through prayer—a turning point in his ministry. After that, Cullis not only used prayer along with medicine, but organized a series of conferences devoted to healing that received tremendous coverage in the press.

Cullis's influence helped to make the healing movement respectable in the eyes of theologians, including Daniel Steele, professor of New Testament at Boston University, and the well-known Baptist theologian A. J. Gordon, founder of Gordon College and author of *The Ministry of Healing: Miracles of Cure in All Ages*.

The healing movement seemed well on its way to being accepted by Protestant Christians in the nineteenth century, but an intellectual backlash led by James Monroe Buckley, editor of the influential Methodist journal, *The Christian Advocate*, served to dampen the growing interest. As the years passed, the nineteenth-century revival of Christian healing was forgotten by theologians and historians, much as the history of healing in the early church had been.

Cઈ

As I became more involved in the healing ministry, I wanted to know more about how we had come from the forgotten nineteenth-century revival of healing to the chaotic explosion of interest in our day. I didn't need to know *why* the interest arose again—it was because people were spiritually hungry and thirsty—but I wanted to know *how* it had come about. So I began to read and try to understand how the twentieth-century revival of interest in spiritual healing had come about and why it had become so controversial and multifaceted.

Unlike the leaders of the short-lived nineteenth-century healing revival, the early Pentecostalists were relatively uneducated evangelists. This did not argue well for their cause with better educated clergy and members of more traditional churches. But the thirst for spiritual healing could not be so easily dampened, and leadership of the late nineteenth-century revival passed to the Pentecostal churches. "Pentecostal," of course, refers to the Day of Pentecost, recorded in the second chapter of Acts, and the gifts of the Spirit bestowed on the disciples, including speaking in tongues and healing.

The disapproval of more intellectual and liberal Christians did not stop the growth of the Pentecostal movement, which had been and continues to be phenomenal. Since it is a movement rather than a denomination, accurate figures are hard to come by, but in the first fifty years of this century the number of Pentecostalists grew to approximately ten million. Today they are by far the fastest growing Christian church in the world.

Although Pentecostalism is now worldwide, it grew to maturity in America. In 1901 at Bethel Bible College in Topeka, Kansas, Charles F. Parham, an itinerant Holiness evangelist and faith-healer, began teaching that speaking in tongues was a necessary part of the "second blessing," or baptism by the Holy Spirit. When he combined this teaching and practice with a healing ministry, Parham began to attract national attention. In 1905 he sent one of his students, an African-American Holiness minister named William Seymour, to Los Angeles, where he held a series of highly successful revivals on Azuza Street, which soon be-

came known as the birthplace of Pentecostalism.[7] Pentecostal churches proliferated.

By the 1940s the ground was laid for what is generally
considered the post-Second World War revival of the healing ministry. Four leaders in this revival were particularly
well known: William Branham, Oral Roberts, Agnes Sanford, and Kathryn Kuhlman.

William Branham was born in 1909 to a fifteen-year-old
mother in a dirt-floored cabin in Kentucky. At nineteen he
began a successful career as a boxer, but a few years later
he experienced a conversion, became an independent
"Holy Ghost" Baptist minister, and launched a ministry of
evangelism. In 1946 he began to focus on healing and,
three years later, Branham was touring Europe to packed
halls. Even greater fame came to him when, in 1951, he
healed Congressman William Upshaw, who had been crippled from birth.

Oral Roberts's parents were Pentecostalists. He was
healed of tuberculosis and a stammer in 1935, and immediately began his long career as an evangelist, though he
did not begin his healing ministry until 1947, a year after
Branham. Roberts reached even greater numbers of people
through his television ministry. In 1965 he founded Oral
Roberts University. Roberts always believed in working
closely with doctors, and in 1981 he established the City
of Faith Medical and Research Center.

The figure who probably influenced—and through her
writings still does today—more leaders in the healing ministry than anyone else is the late Agnes Sanford. The

---

7. The rise of the Pentecostal churches under William Seymour's
leadership and with both white and black members slowly and sadly
dissolved into primarily white and primarily black congregations and
denominations. For a detailed account, read Harvey Cox, *Fire from
Heaven: The Rise of Pentecostal Spirituality and the Reshaping of Religion in
the Twenty-first Century* (Reading, Mass.: Addison Wesley, 1995).

daughter of Presbyterian missionaries to China, she married Episcopal priest Edgar Sanford in 1923. Her first book, *The Healing Light*, was published in that watershed year of 1947, and in 1955 she and her husband started the School of Pastoral Care, offering resident conferences for clergy and their wives. These conferences continue today. Her deep faith and outstanding teaching ability left a lasting impression on thousands.

All of these leading figures certainly believed that healing was God's work and not their own, but no one stated this more strongly than Kathryn Kuhlman. She greatly resented being called a faith-healer and said, "I have no healing power. I never healed anyone. I am absolutely dependent upon the power of the Holy Spirit." Like Branham and Roberts, Kuhlman started as an evangelist and later began to focus on healing. She had only a tenth-grade education, saying that the Holy Spirit was the only teacher she ever had. In 1968 she published an immensely popular book entitled *I Believe in Miracles*, which was ghost-written by an Episcopalian reporter, Emily Gardiner Neal.

In 1962, at the Second Vatican Council, the Roman Catholic Church revised its official attitude toward healing. The "last rites" continued to be a sacrament, but healing was brought out of obscurity when Roman Catholics rediscovered their church's traditions of healing prayer for the sick. This change of attitude swept through the Roman Catholic Church in the 1960s.

In the meantime, Kathryn Kuhlman had settled in Los Angeles and was speaking to seven thousand people a week. Increasingly these audiences began to come from all denominations; they wanted not to become Pentecostalists, but to take healing back to their own churches. Thus, among Catholic and other denominations the charismatic movement was born.

In addition to these Pentecostal/charismatic develop-
ments, the twentieth-century ministry of healing arose in a
number of independent movements. The most major of
these started in the 1930s, when two Episcopalians, Ethel
Tulloch Banks and John Gaynor Banks, founded the Order
of Saint Luke. This international organization of laity and
clergy interested in Christian healing has grown and flour-
ished since that time. Originally Episcopalian, it soon became ecumenical and there are many active chapters today.
Although there may be charismatic members, the organization is not primarily a part of the Pentecostal/charismatic
tradition.

☃

What lies ahead for the healing revival? I was interested
to read of what had happened in the 1980s at Fuller Seminary, a Bible-centered, ecumenical seminary in Pasadena,
California. In 1982, Peter Wagner and John Wimber
joined forces to teach a course in healing there called
"Signs, Wonders and Church Growth." They had both a
presentation and a practicum; in the practicum portion
there were both physical and emotional healings and a
strong sense of God's presence. Now many conservative,
Bible-based evangelicals have a tradition, stemming from
the Reformation, that the time for healing is over. The
class ran for four years but then the controversy engen-
dered by it (particularly the practicum—healings *happened!*)
caused Fuller to cancel the class (which by then had become famous) while the administration studied the situ-
ation and revised the course.

One of the professors in the course, John Wimber, left
to found the Vineyard Fellowship, a nationwide network of
congregations emphasizing the gifts of the Spirit. He and

Peter Wagner claim in their books and speeches that we are at the start of a "third wave," following the waves of the Pentecostal and charismatic revivals: an increased emphasis on an openness to God's power to heal, to guide, and to convert. Wagner writes that the major variation in the "third wave"

> comes in the understanding of the meaning of baptism in the Holy Spirit and the role of tongues in authenticating this. I myself, for example, would rather not have people call me a charismatic....I am simply an evangelical Congregationalist who is open to the Holy Spirit working through me and my church in any way he chooses.[8]

Perhaps someday both healing and prayer will be generally accepted as seminary subjects as well as topics to be taught in every parish. In the Episcopal Church, at the General Theological Seminary in New York, the dean, Bishop Craig Anderson, has recently inaugurated a class in healing. In Tilden Edwards's words, "This seems a ripe and important historical moment for overcoming the schizophrenia present at least since the Middle Ages in our approaches to the knowledge of God and maturation of the Christian life."[9]

---

8. C. Peter Wagner, *The Third Wave of the Holy Spirit* (Ann Arbor: Vine Press/Servant Publications, 1988), pp. 18-19.
9. Tilden H. Edwards, Jr., "Spiritual Formation in Theological Schools: Ferment and Challenge," *Theological Education*, vol. 17 (Autumn, 1980), p. 20.

The Landscape
of Prayer

A landscape is something we see. Landscapes can be
meadows, city streets, or four walls. Looked at more
broadly, landscapes are not just what can be framed in a
photograph, but also the whole moving panorama of life
around us. No two people will look at the same landscape
in exactly the same way because we also have an interior
landscape of meaning—or lack of meaning—that influences
how we see what is around us.

"If we knew how to listen to God, if we knew how to
look around us, our whole life would become prayer,"[1]
wrote Abbé Michel Quoist in his book, *Prayers*. He obviously didn't mean just *prayers*—words that we say to
God—but something much broader and deeper. Funda-
mentally, *prayer* (without the "s") means any communication or communion with God. And "a life of prayer" means
that we are in constant communion with God. Or trying to
be so.

For over forty years I have been "trying to be so." Thirty
of these years I have been a spiritual director, someone
who helps others to be in communion with God. I also
spend six weeks a year as an oblate in a monastery, and I
have taught prayer and written about prayer. Obviously
this interior landscape of prayer affects the way I see the

---

1. Michel Quoist, *Prayers*, trans. Agnes M. Forsyth and Anne Marie de
Commaille (New York: Sheed & Ward, 1963), p. 30.

world around me, including how I see healing prayer. When I view healing prayer from my interior landscape, I see it as very natural because it is cut from the same piece of cloth as a life of prayer. Healing prayer reminds us as ministers of healing that what is most important is not exactly how we pray for healing, but being in communion with God when we do so.

Recently a group of us from Saint Luke's went to hear a series of lectures by Jeffrey Satinover, M.D., medical director of a nearby Jungian Institute, on "Psychosomatic Illness and the Judeo-Christian Tradition." After presenting a detailed history of medical attitudes toward psychosomatic illness, he spoke about magic. Magic, in Satinover's terms, was not just stage magic. He used the word very broadly and deeply to cover anything where human beings think that they should try to be in control. In this sense, he said, all medicine is magic.

Indeed, when I thought about it, the underlying theme of our western culture is magic. We want to be in control, to manipulate life to fit our desires. In contrast, a Judeo-Christian perspective assumes that God is in control. As we surrender to God and follow God's lead in our lives, we are healed. We may or may not be physically cured, but we are healed in the sense that our lives are in God's hands and we know it. Whatever our physical condition, we are at peace. Physical cures in response to prayer obviously happen, but not for everyone. But all of us, with time, prayer, and surrender to God, may be *healed*.

My friend Martha had a directee, Helen, who was dying of a brain tumor. Helen wanted prayers for physical healing. Every week for a year and a half one or two of us from the healing team prayed for and with Helen. There was no improvement in her physical condition. Indeed, her brain tumor grew steadily worse. But during the same time her spiritual growth was tremendous. A few days before Helen died, when she could talk only with difficulty, she said to me, in a clear but halting voice: "Now when I pray...I don't pray *to* God....I pray *with* God."

When I am teaching prayer I often use Helen's words as an illustration of the *unitive stage,* or *union with God,* traditionally the highest stage of the spiritual life. Helen was no longer *asking God* for something; she was simply praying *with* God.

All of us in our healing group at Saint Luke's found that our spiritual lives deepened as we prayed for people, not only people whose conditions were as remarkable as Helen's, but for anyone. Healing puts both the one who prays and the one being prayed for in touch with God. Slowly our own work becomes less and God's work becomes more. This process of growth in prayer is well illustrated by an analogy made by Saint Teresa of Avila. In the beginning, she says, the garden of the soul is watered by lowering a bucket on a rope down the well. Hand over hand it is pulled up and carried to the garden. A windlas makes it easier, and then a great improvement: a system of irrigation is installed. And finally, it rains.

⚬ẞ

My study of the history of healing revealed to me how the rise and persistence of rational thinking had relegated healing to the periphery of the church, but it also made me realize that the study and teaching of *all* prayer has been neglected for the same reason. Healing was—and is—often treated by the rest of the family like a disreputable relative, while the study and teaching of prayer has simply been ignored.

Our church meetings and publications argue endlessly over what is making our churches decline. We have a great tendency not to see the forest for the trees. The church is built on communication and communion with Christ, and will fail for the lack of it. It is prayer, not winning argu- ꭓ ments, that will save the church from decline. Prayer is what enlivens us as individuals and what enlivens the church. The liturgical *form* of our prayer together helps, but unless the liturgy is infused with the deep prayer of both clergy and congregation it will be as "sounding brass."

The people of God need to be people of prayer, people whose interior landscapes have been formed by personal prayer and prayerful reading of Scripture. And certainly, the priests of God need to be people of prayer whose pub- lic prayers spring from their own landscape of prayer and who sprinkle the church services with prayerful silence to allow room for all present to listen to God.

Morton Kelsey, in words that I wish were taken to heart and practice by all churches and seminaries, speaks of this need for training in prayer, both in our seminaries and in our parishes:

> People do not learn to deal with the infinitely profound depth of God and the spiritual world all by themselves. We don't put students in a classroom and tell them to come up with differential and integral calculus. They need to be taught. Each church needs to provide classes in forms of prayer. This is only possible if seminaries are training pastors in prayer, contemplation and meditation, and group process.
>
> In addition, each Christian fellowship needs to provide prayer groups led by informed Christians in which people can share their spiritual lives and religious experiences and pray together. These informal prayer groups will give life

and body to formal preaching and sacramental services of the church.[2]

When I tell lay people that prayer is seldom taught in seminaries, they are invariably surprised if not disbelieving. Their assumption is that "of course prayer is taught in seminaries." And so some of them trustingly go to their pastors for spiritual direction or ask them to teach a group how to pray. In a landmark study reported in the journal *Theological Education*, Tilden Edwards noted that most seminaries do little toward the spiritual formation of future clergy. In addition, he stated that it is

> increasingly abnormal for students entering most schools to have been exposed to a mutually reinforcing, significant set of spiritual formational forces from family, friends, pastor, church, school, work, and larger cultural influences. Instead, many come fresh from recent conversion experiences with little history in the church, or from conflicting or "flabby" religious backgrounds....They have not been exposed to classical spiritual disciplines or to a serious religious community's rhythm and way of life.[3]

It was to address that need that the Annand Program of Spiritual Growth at Yale/Berkeley Divinity Schools in New Haven was started. Here I discovered a program addressing the very issues that had become of concern to me, and in 1992 I accepted their invitation to become a mentor in the program. The Annand Program is extracurricular and ecumenical. Students get no credit and pay no fee. Instead,

---

2. Morton Kelsey, "The Former Age and the New Age: The Perennial Quest for the Spiritual Life," *New Age Spirituality*, ed. Duncan Ferguson (Louisville, Ky.: Westminster/John Knox, 1993), p. 57.
3. Tilden H. Edwards, Jr., "Spiritual Formation in Theological Schools: Ferment and Challenge," *Theological Education*, vol. 17 (Autumn, 1980), p. 20.

mentors lead small groups on prayer and allied subjects. To me the most important subject was the most basic and I volunteered to teach an *Introduction to Prayer and Meditation* group as well as a group on healing.

♋

Whether clergy or lay, if you want to introduce a healing ministry in your parish, remember that healing is part of the landscape of prayer. It may spring from that landscape or it may lead to that landscape, but it cannot be separated from that landscape. Healing is not just another program. Those who lead the ministry will need to give themselves more generously to God in prayer and to be more open about it to those they lead.

I have taught prayer to parish groups for many years and it might be helpful to those who are thinking of starting a healing and prayer group if I share something about how I teach classes on prayer.

I am always assaulted by feelings of inadequacy as I prepare to teach, which is just as well because it turns me to a deeper commitment to my own life of prayer. Without it I could not teach. We can learn a great deal about prayer from books, but books are never a substitute for praying.

For the first session (after an opening prayer) I usually begin a new group by asking people how they might define prayer. There are many definitions that could be offered, but usually someone will say something like "communication with God." I'm apt to add "and silent communion with God." If other good definitions have been offered I affirm them but suggest that we concentrate on these simple ones to start with.

Then, equipped with an easel, pad, and magic marker, I ask people to tell me all the different ways it is possible to pray they can think of.

"In words," says one, and I write it down.

"Silently."

"By singing?" And I affirm them.

We continue with a long list, which usually contains dance, kneeling, with the Bible, praying alone, in church, while jogging, reading or praying prayers written by someone else, and more. Someone is fairly sure to suggest thanksgiving or confession, and I point out that they are *subjects* of prayer and not *ways* of prayer.

When I teach I bring with me copies of the following list of ways of praying, and I usually hand them out at this point.

Ways of Praying[4]

In Common Language	In Traditional Terms
Conversational prayer	Colloquy
Praying together in Christ —in church —in other people's words	Corporate prayer
Praying during the eucharist or Holy Communion	Liturgical, sacramental prayer
Listening prayer	Mental prayer practicing spiritual exercises or methods of meditation that use the imagination

---

4. May be reproduced for parish use if the following credit is given: From *Healing in the Landscape of Prayer* by Avery Brooke (Cambridge, Mass.: Cowley Publications, 1996).

Prayerful reading of the Bible and spiritual books	*Lectio divina*
Praying with one's feelings	Affective prayer
A turning of the will and attention	An act of recollection
Use of the body in prayer	
Symbolic dedication of activities to God	Sacramental living
Preparation for deeper prayer by repeating short prayers such as the Jesus Prayer or mantras, using the rosary or icons, practicing Centering Prayer	The work of contemplation
Wordless prayer —your own —God's prayer in you	Contemplation —Simple —Infused

I tell the group that knowing the traditional terms will make it easier for them to understand many other books on prayer that use these terms, but if the terms are not familiar that does not mean they do not know much about prayer. People usually find they know more about praying than they think they do, and this interior knowing is the foundation on which to build what they learn. In practice, ways of prayer cross border lines. Lists of definitions and terms are just an aid to understanding. Listening prayer, for instance, keeps our prayer from being a monologue and can be a part of any other form of prayer if we pause to listen.

I always have praying together be a part of any session. Often it is just five to fifteen minutes in silence to use as the Spirit moves each individual, but for the first session I usually lead the group in about ten minutes of silent conversational prayer, explaining beforehand that now we turn to the classic *subjects* of prayer: *adoration, confession, thanksgiving, intercession,* and *petition.* (There are other ways of naming these but I find this listing most useful.) I say a few words of prayer or bidding, followed by a few minutes of silent prayer. It is important that my own words are either prayer or prayerful, informal and extemporaneous. For instance, I don't say, "I invite your prayers of adoration," but something like, "Take a few moments to tell God how you love him or her." If it comes more naturally to say "I love you, Jesus," then I do so.

Sometimes I lead the prayers by actually praying. Then I might say something like: "I love you, God. I love you for giving me life. [silence] I love you through and for many things in the world you have made." Then, after several more minutes of silence, "I love you for forgiving me [pause] again and again," followed by more silence. And then on through the other traditional subjects.

It is hard, even after all these years, to let others catch a real glimpse of me at a deeper and more vulnerable level than usual. And of course, this is just the point. Unless I can show the group that prayer is both real and intimate to me (or that I am trying to make it so), I can't teach prayer.

For my second meeting with a group, I usually open with ten minutes of silent prayer. I don't tell people how to use the time, but leave that to the Holy Spirit. I then introduce the idea of having a relationship with God. Such a relationship is the basis of all prayer: contemplation, meditation, and centering prayer all play their part in the life of prayer, but a relationship with God is the foundation. In it we learn to love God and to know we are loved. We learn to listen, to argue, to obey, to disobey, to be forgiven. In the process we learn to pray.

I always invite members of the group to share any experiences of relating to God that they have had and share one or two myself. I ask if they can describe a time when they have felt very close to God. Has prayer been a one-way street, or do they sometimes receive answers from God? How? We discuss hearing God through Scripture passages coming home to us and through everyday and major events in our lives.

If the discussion is going well, I keep it going to the end. If it slows down I save half an hour and end with the following spiritual exercise.

On a large pad I make three columns. Above the first I write "Daily"; above the center column I write "Weekly"; and above the third column, "Less Frequently." I tell them that these headings are for any kinds of prayer or spiritual aids or disciplines that they do or know of. I try to get quite a full sheet. Among the possibilities I have found are those listed on the following page.

Daily	Weekly	Less Frequently
Quick prayer when rising in the morning and before bed	Sunday church: eucharist, Holy Communion, mass	Retreats or quiet days, either alone or with others
Grace at meals	Midweek services	Spiritual direction
Daily office, reading a devotional pamphlet or book	Visiting those who are sick or in need	Keeping the feasts and fasts of the church year
Conversational prayer, centering prayer, wordless prayer	Prayer or study groups	Spiritual disciplines, such as fasting, confession
Prayerful Bible reading		

I don't share these lists with the group, but have the items in mind to help coax answers if responses are slow. When the sheet is full of ideas I give everyone paper and pencil and say "You are all going to have ten minutes to consider, with God, what your personal Rule of Prayer should be." I explain that a Rule of Prayer is not a *law* but something you do *as a rule*. I urge them to be practical rather than committing themselves to an ideal they cannot keep, and tell them that ten or fifteen minutes of daily conversational prayer is a good way to start. We then enter the ten minutes of silence with God.

I always teach that prayer is the easiest thing in the world to do but also the hardest. It is the easiest because all you have to do is turn toward God and start praying. It is the hardest because we always have something to do that seems more important (absurd but true). Making a habit of prayer takes stubborn persistence. Like painting, dance, music, or medicine, prayer and healing prayer are both arts, and we must practice them to learn them. Once people have started praying regularly through the group's weekly support, my task as a teacher is half done; the Holy Spirit is the real teacher of prayer and will take over from there.

It takes many weeks to get to that point, however, and during that time we may all read and discuss suitable books. (A list of suggested readings is provided at the back of this book.) There is much to learn about prayer that is of an academic nature: How have others prayed in the Christian tradition? How does prayer enliven theology and theology enliven prayer? What are the great, classic writings in spirituality? What are the meanings—in the common language of today—of obscure or archaic words used in those classic writings? When I choose to use a book in a group, I always save time to pray and to discuss how prayer is going for people in their daily lives.

ᴄꙅ

Academic studies concentrate on learning *about* God and about other people's relationships with God, while prayer concentrates on our *own* relationship with God. Prayer enlivens our studies. Our studies guide and inform our prayer. In the groups of seminarians studying prayer that I mentored in the Annand Program in New Haven we had to crowd in presentation, discussion, and practicum in an hour and a half a week. The presentation was about different kinds of prayer and meditation, the practicum was doing them, and the discussion was whatever the students needed to discuss. We wished there had been time to assign reading. We wished more students had time to come. But it was a beginning.

My healing group at Yale fell into the same pattern of presentation, discussion, and practicum. There was, however, a significant difference. Healing prayer itself has an immediate demand. We are not slowly and silently building a relationship with God in prayer; we are asking God in our own words, out loud and in front of our peers, to *do* something. Practicing healing prayer plunges us into a relationship with God.

In class I try to approach this gently. In the first session we don't lay on hands but just do intercessory prayer out loud as the Spirit moves. Some students are used to this kind of prayer, but for others it is an effort. "Try to say more than just a name," I tell them.

Some prayers are spoken easily, and some shyly and with effort. "For my old friend Jane, who has just discovered she has cancer."

"For Timothy, who is having trouble with his faith."

"For those in prison, particularly Michael and his family."

Afterwards a student may say, with a touch of surprise, "I've never prayed extemporaneously before."

As time goes on they become more comfortable in asking prayers for themselves and each other. They come to trust the confidentiality in the group and dare to pray for personal matters: "I'd like prayers for my marriage, please."

By this time they would have learned that a gentle question in response, such as, "Is there anything special about your marriage that you need prayers for?", may seem called for, but prying and advice giving are never right. We are asking help from *God,* not from our amateur selves.

When we turn to prayer for physical healing for each other, our relationship with God deepens in a different way. Here is an immediate need of a classmate we have become close to. We ourselves are powerless to help and compassion opens us to God. We dare to believe that God can help—and ask.

One day a student in one of my classes on healing prayer asked prayers for his friend Mike: "He'd hardly gotten settled into his first year in seminary when one eye got badly hit by a squash ball. The eye is damaged and filled with blood and he can't see out of it. It is impossible for him to read, as moving his good eye causes the other to move and results in a good deal of pain."

And so we laid hands on Mike's friend and prayed with him for Mike. A week or so later Mike himself turned up at our group asking if we could pray for his mother. I said, "Of course," and we laid hands on Mike and prayed with him for his mother, who had cancer. While we were at it we again prayed for his eye. At the end of our time together Mike asked if he could join the group. Again I said, "Of course."

In the meanwhile the doctors had done a minor operation on Mike's eye. It improved for four or five days but then regressed. One day Mike told us that the doctors decided a more serious operation was needed. "They want," he said, "to cut a new channel to drain the blood and aqueous fluid out of my eye. Next week I have to go in for a pre-operative check-up."

"Look," I said, "we haven't done any soaking prayer yet. How would you feel, Mike, if we did fifteen minutes of prayer for your eye?"

"That would be fine."

So I chose someone to lay hands on his head and pray out loud. "Just pray briefly," I told them, "and we'll spend the rest of the time in silence."

The group gathered round, laying hands on Mike or on the shoulder or back of the one who spoke our prayer. It seemed to me a bit frightening for a student to lay a hand on his eyes: I wasn't sure they were ready. So, after asking Mike if it was all right and receiving his assent, I laid my own hand over his eye and the prayer was said. A few minutes into the silence I was moved by the Spirit to pick up his friend's hand and put it over Mike's eye. I then laid my hand over his friend's hand and continued to pray. At the end of fifteen minutes of silent prayer I said, "Amen." Slowly people removed their hands. No one spoke. At least one person was crying.

That week Mike went for the pre-operative check-up. The infusion of blood was receding and his sight had started to come back. The doctor canceled the operation.

In class the next week there was much gratitude to God and a quiet awe about what had happened. But from a teaching point of view what probably mattered most is that the students had dared to pray and had experienced that prayer together. They grew in faith and they grew in their relationship with God. Healing prayer had taken its proper place as part of the landscape of prayer.

Developing a
Healing Ministry

E arly in my ministry at Saint Luke's I began to attend a variety of healing conferences and missions. Some were charismatic and evangelical, such as those led by Francis and Judith MacNutt. Prayer and praise songs abounded, beautiful singing in tongues arose spontaneously, and people fell to the floor, "slain in the Spirit." I urged others of our group to attend, but some were completely turned off. The Order of Saint Luke offered services nearer to our desires, but it was the Episcopal Healing Ministry Foundation, founded by the late Emily Gardiner Neal, whose teachings and style seemed most suitable for mainline churches. Standard hymns replaced prayer and praise songs, and a contagious openness to the Spirit replaced speaking in tongues.

Unfortunately, the Foundation has become inactive since Mrs. Neal's death, but before she died I met her protégée, Irene Perkins. Irene is a registered nurse and a compelling speaker, and I was moved by hearing her. A year later I was unexpectedly asked to lead a conference on healing, and I persuaded Irene to lead it with me. We found that we worked wonderfully well together, and we have led conferences together ever since.

Healing conferences tend to be ecumenical, and as I began leading conferences in cities scattered across the United States, as well as going to conferences held by others, I became aware of the extent and variety of the healing movement. These experiences, together with my work at Saint Luke's and my mentoring groups of seminarians at Yale, formed a rich seedbed for my developing thoughts about healing.

My approach to healing and the way that a healing ministry has emerged at Saint Luke's are not patterns that will work for all churches, but we have learned some possibly useful things I would like to share.

✆

Let us presume for the moment that you are a clergy person wishing to develop a healing ministry in your church. What are your choices? The simplest way is the priestly one where, in the context of a regular weekday or a special service, the clergy anoint, lay on hands, and pray for those who desire prayer, using traditional or extemporaneous prayers.

The major problem with this priestly way is that it leaves out the laity. Once you've aroused interest in the ministry of healing, a lay member of your congregation may well come to you and say that they have a gift for healing, or just that they want to help. How do you respond? Well, you could ask him or her to lay a hand on your shoulder and/or the shoulder of the person being prayed for and to pray silently with you as a partner. You could then invite those who seem truly called to a healing ministry to join you in praying aloud.

This is a relatively simple solution, but there is a drawback: other lay people may volunteer and not all of them may seem suitable for this ministry. Thinking through this problem, you may decide that you will say "No" to all lay participation. But in so doing you may be denying someone the opportunity to follow a genuine prompting of the Holy Spirit in a ministry that has been, more often than not, lay-led for centuries.

But—theologically—*should* it be lay-led? And should the laity lay on hands in services? There are Christians who believe that Jesus' call to his disciples to heal was meant just for those disciples, who were prototypes for the priesthood (see Matt. 10:1; Mark 6:7; Luke 10:1). These same Christians would point to the passage in James that reads, "Are any among you sick? They should call for the *elders* of the church and have them pray over them, anointing them with oil in the name of the Lord" (5:14) and translate "elders" as "presbyters." But was Paul talking only to presbyters (or elders) when he wrote his wonderful passage in 1 Corinthians 12 on many gifts but one body? And was Jesus calling only his first disciples to heal? To me it seems unlikely, and early church history clearly implies the involvement of the laity in the healing ministry.

The revival of healing in our own century is new enough that traditions are still in formation and sometimes even in conflict. In the Episcopal Church, for instance, while the *Book of Common Prayer* has a short section on Ministration to the Sick, it refers only to the *priest* (and not members of the laity) laying on hands. *The Book of Occasional Services* is slightly broader and allows for "lay persons with a gift of healing" to join the priest in the laying on of hands.[1] But in practice, Episcopal laity have been laying on hands for much of this century, not to mention during that ill-fated revival of the nineteenth century.

The Report of the Joint Commission on the Ministry of Healing to the General Convention of the Episcopal Church, written in 1964 and thus predating both the 1979

---

1. *The Book of Common Prayer* (1979), pp. 453-461 and *The Book of Occasional Services* (New York: Church Pension Fund, 1988), p. 166.

Book of Common Prayer and *The Book of Occasional Services*, includes these strong words calling for the inclusion of the laity in the healing ministry:

> The prayer of a righteous man is always acceptable. If the Church refuses to acknowledge such a ministry or insists on smugly proclaiming that the Apostolic Ministry is sufficient, unlimited, and exclusively all-powerful for all purposes, then those called by God the Holy Ghost will be forced to exercise their ministry outside the Church....
>
> If the healing ministry is not taught and practiced within the Church, people will go where it is being taught and practiced (and often over-emphasized, to the exclusion of the rest of the Gospel)....
>
> The Church should make full use of such lay ministry and give to such ministers training, guidance, direction, and support....
>
> It must therefore, be recognized by the Church that both priest and people must be caught up in this life-giving, life-mending experience, thus participating in the all-inclusive ministry of reconciliation. These, then, are the ministers of healing.[2]

The convention unanimously adopted statements reflecting the heart of this report.

No matter who is leading the healing ministry of a congregation—laity or clergy—it has been my experience that close clergy involvement in and authority over parish healing ministries is a wise safeguard that is of great benefit to all, as I hope to show.

---

2. From the special edition reprinted by The Episcopal Healing Ministry Foundation of the *Report of the Joint Commission on the Ministry of Healing to the General Convention of the Episcopal Church, St. Louis, Mo., 1964, with Resolutions Adopted* (Cincinnati, 1987), p. 12.

CR

A parish ministry of healing starts when someone feels a quiet call from the Spirit to "do something about healing." This "someone" is often a member of the clergy but may well be a lay person. If the initial call comes to a clergy person, I suggest that the best lay people to turn to are those who are already involved in a prayer group. Failing that, you could choose those parishioners who seem to you to be the most prayerful and then put out a call to the parish as a whole for anyone else who might be interested in learning about healing.

It is probably wise not to talk about "training a healing team" at first. Some good candidates may be scared off and some unsuitable candidates attracted. Just call it "a workshop to learn more about healing." When you have worked with people for some time you will have a better idea who is ready to lay on hands in the name of the church.

If your parish is very small, you may find yourselves in a group of three. If so, learning will go faster, but if you wish to have more people in the group you might reach outside the parish by advertising in the local paper. Healing often attracts the unchurched.

Once you have a group, what do you teach and learn? We began at Saint Luke's by studying a book together. I recommend several possibilities in the suggestions for further reading section at the back. This book might also be useful. Healing and prayer should be quite central to whatever book, or books, you choose to start with. A group could also profitably spend several weeks reading and discussing the healing stories in the Bible. Once your group has a solid base of understanding, then you can read books on specialized subjects. Expect all books to cause controversy but don't be concerned, as this makes for lively discussion.

The information found in books is important but the most important learning has to do with prayer. I always save twenty minutes to a half-hour (out of an hour and a half) for prayer. First of all, most people are shy about praying out loud and extemporaneously. I find it wise to begin gently with intercessions. The forms given for the Prayers of the People in the *Book of Common Prayer* (or a similar form for intercessory prayer) are useful here.[3] I adapt them slightly and say both the bidding and the prayer, leaving time between them for personal intercessions. I suggest that instead of just mentioning names they say something of the individuals and their needs. People will usually need encouragement—and long intervals of silence—to speak prayers out loud.

After concentrating on intercession for a couple of meetings, it is time to begin laying hands on each other while praying. I described some of this process of learning earlier, but it is worth emphasizing: *What you are trying to learn is how to forget yourself and concentrate on God and the person you are praying for.* You hand over your self-consciousness, your worry about "doing it right," and your concern about not failing the sick person to God. *You* don't do it at all, God does. You just offer yourself as a channel for God's healing grace.

Healing prayers are said "in the name of Jesus Christ." I usually start my prayer by saying, "I lay my hands upon you in the name of Jesus Christ, our Lord and Savior." It is a salutary reminder that *we* are not the healers. What does it mean to do something "in the name of"? It means to do

---

3. See the resource section at the end of this book for prayers and a litany of healing, healing services, a service of commissioning, and suggestions for hymns that are appropriate for healing services.

something under and with their authority. As baptized Christians we have that authority and we are called to use it. Some of us are more gifted in healing than others, but all of us are called to pray for healing.

How did Jesus heal? Is there a pattern to follow? No, except that he said to heal in his name, and he healed simply and without fanfare. Sometimes he just stated, "You are healed." Sometimes he touched them and sometimes people touched him. Sometimes the person was not even present. The faith of the people involved played a part—certainly Jesus' faith did. The sick person might have faith, or the faith might be that of the person's friends or family, but faith certainly helped. Jesus said more than once, "Your faith has healed you." Sometimes he told them to do something—to eat, to show themselves to the priests, to pick up their bed and walk, to go and sin no more. Sometimes he said nothing.

The act of laying on hands is not something Jesus routinely did to accomplish healing. His practice was so varied that it almost seems he varied it purposely so we could not copy it, imbue the act itself with power, and try to possess it. Healing came through Jesus not because of a particular rite but because he was constantly in touch with God.

Why then do we lay on hands at all? We do because it is a sacramental act symbolizing God's healing grace coming through us to the one we are praying for. We lay on hands because we pray with all of our being, including our bodies, not just our words. The laying on of hands leaves room for silent prayer and silence leaves more room for God.

It is important to read books, to hear an occasional speaker on healing, to go to healing missions or conferences, but it is the *practice* of healing prayer that is at the heart of preparation for the healing ministry. How long should this preparation go on? My instinctive response to this question is "Forever!" And there is truth in that, but in practice we have found that a year's preparation—starting with an eight-week study group—works well. Irene Perkins's home parish of Saint Benedict's in Plantation, Florida, starts with an eight- to ten-week course, followed by a period of apprenticeship, though this pattern may change with new leadership. Saint Thomas' Church in Cincinnati requires prospective team members to "participate in a training program that will include both theoretical and practical elements." This includes "an apprenticeship of at least forty sessions."

Is such a long training necessary? For some perhaps not, but certainly the chances of having a wonderfully knowledgeable, wise, and Christ-centered group will be increased if it is required. Once they are trained they can train others. And certainly, as we learned in our School for Christian Healing, such a prayerful and committed a group of disciples is a marvelous vehicle for evangelism.

Such training and preparation takes time and trouble to achieve, but if you have a lay healing team with clergy supervision and cooperation the lengthy process has great advantages. I have had a number of clergy call and ask what they should do about unsuitable lay people who feel they are called to the healing ministry and want to be active in the parish. Often with a note of desperation in their voice they ask, "What should I *say* to them?"

If you have a trained lay healing team with a requirement of at least a year's study and experience, the answer is simple: say that everyone who feels called to the ministry must work, study, and pray with the healing group for at least a year. When both the group and the clergy think the new candidate is ready, he or she may be commissioned to join the healing team. If the members of the group are themselves trained and experienced, then the new candidate will learn from their community wisdom as well as from any studies required.

The participation of the clergy in study with a lay group need not continue beyond the original six or eight weeks, but clergy should keep in close touch with the healing group. No matter how deeply lay people are involved in the healing ministry, when it is done in a church service or in the name of the parish it is the responsibility of the clergy to see that it is done well. It is rare, thank God, but I have heard horror stories of untrained, unsupervised, and enthusiastic ministers of healing claiming that a person's illness is cured and telling them to throw away their medicine and not go back to the doctor. Almost as bad are lay ministers who blame the patient for not becoming well and say things like, "You must have a block between you and God or you would be well now." (Just what a person with cancer needs to hear.) There is also danger, in this litigious age, if ministers lay on hands when alone with a person; they should always work in pairs. And it is all too easy to forget that it is our *prayers* that are being called for, not our advice, counsel, or amateur psychologizing.

With a trained lay team that is accountable to clergy and to each other, there is a strong protection against such excesses. I have known of parishes where wise clergy have recognized the call and giftedness of a single lay person, sent her to healing conferences, asked her to complete suitable studies, and then appointed her to help in the parish healing ministry. If lay ministers pray extemporaneously the need for training is more obvious, but even if lay assistants do nothing but pray silently I believe that they need training if we believe that silent prayer has any significance—and surely it does.

◌

Healing services take many forms and, although I am writing as an Episcopalian, I am very conscious of the varied practices and traditions of other denominations. But no matter what the denomination, many aspects of a healing service are of common concern.

Let me consider with you first a service where a priest anoints people in the context of the eucharist. I have seen a service where those wishing healing prayer were asked to come forward in the midst of the Sunday service. Since this is a bit daunting, only a few came forward—hence the service was not unduly lengthened. The priest then anointed them and prayed traditional prayers. Two lay persons assisted by laying hands on the priest's shoulders and praying silently. It was all done with great dignity and beauty and was very moving.

A similar service is held once a month in the context of the eucharist at the monastery of the Holy Cross, where I am an oblate. The celebrant invites those who desire prayer to come forward, asks what they wish prayer for, lays on hands, and prays extemporaneously. As he prays he is supported by the prayers of the whole congregation, who all gather to pray and to lay hands on the people in front of them. It is a powerful service. The major drawback to this model is that it is very public. A person wishing healing for their marriage, for instance, is sometimes shy of coming forward.

More commonly, a priest who wishes to anoint or lay on hands for healing will do so in a small, weekday service. After receiving communion those who seek healing may simply stay at the rail when others return to their seats. This will only work if there are no more people than will fill the rail, or if there is a second priest, deacon, or lay minister following after the chalice bearer to lay on hands. An alternative is to have a short and separate healing service immediately after the service of eucharist. Prayers may be used from the *Book of Common Prayer* (pages 453-460) or from A Public Service of Healing in *The Book of Occasional Services* (pages 162-169).

Both of these choices have obvious drawbacks. To have people stay at the rail if they wish healing is apt to be confusing, and to lay on hands after the eucharist is over makes it seem that it is not a part of the service. You also do not want to force those who have come to that midweek eucharist for years into a service of healing they may not wish to attend. However, if a church has never had a midweek eucharist, it should be possible to start one with healing incorporated from the beginning. If a second midweek eucharist is desired, it could incorporate healing.

At Saint Luke's the clergy offered a healing service after the midweek eucharist long before lay members were trained to assist and it has remained a clergy-led service, with the occasional help of a lay minister. At present, clergy and the lay healing team cooperate in a once-a-month healing service on Sunday evenings at 5 p.m. We hope to institute monthly healing services at one of the Sunday morning eucharists soon.

Healing for everyone in the context of regular Sunday services may be desirable but is often difficult. I was present at one such occasion when Irene Perkins had been asked to preach and lay on hands. It was profoundly moving to see members of the large congregation, from age eight to eighty, streaming up the aisle. But it was also exhausting. If each individual prayer adds just a minute to the service, thirty people add thirty minutes, sixty people add an hour, and one is soon facing an impossibly long service. Obviously, the more people you have laying on hands the more you can shorten the time, but then you need room for a good number of stations for healing.

An alternative that works well but is not available in all churches is to have a healing station in a side chapel. People may slip into the chapel on their way back from communion. If the church's side aisles are wide enough you can have lay healing teams stationed there, although this seldom affords enough privacy. One way successfully done in some churches is to have the celebrant invite the lay ministers forward before the singing of the last hymn. They face the altar and sing until the dismissal and then take stations on the other side of the rail. People who wish healing prayers come forward as others leave and then leave themselves. The way we hope to do it at Saint Luke's is to reserve a section of the pews in the back of the church where people may go for healing prayer either before or after receiving communion.

The question of privacy is very important, and consideration should be given to having stations where people will not be overheard. The need for privacy can be avoided by not asking what people want healing for and just praying a set prayer. But this takes away a major aspect of the healing ministry. When people bring forward their deepest need and brokenness, voice it out loud, and receive the caring response of a representative of the church, the act of verbalizing what is troubling them is in itself a powerful healing agent. As Roman Catholic priest Leo Thomas says, the minister of healing is, in the eyes of the one prayed for, "a bearer of Christ, a living sacrament."[4] Outside of the sacrament of reconciliation (or confession), the church offers nothing similar that is simultaneously liturgical and so deeply personal. It is a precious combination.

---

4. Leo Thomas, OP, and Jan Alkire, *Healing as a Parish Ministry* (Notre Dame, Ind.: Ave Maria Press, 1992).

With privacy from being overheard ensured, there remains the need to stress the fact that all ministers of healing keep what has been said to them in complete confidence. This should be so well instilled that it becomes part of their very nature.

CR

Our healing service at Saint Luke's is within the service of the Holy Eucharist in the *Book of Common Prayer.* We have worked out an order of officiants, with additional prayers and informal rubrics. The lay ministers, as described earlier, have all had at least one year's training, have been approved by the clergy, and have been commissioned in a special service. On the day of a service in which they will lay on hands the lay ministers are asked to spend a quiet day and arrive a half hour early to pray silently in the chapel.

Although some of our group rather like the joyous prayer and praise songs usually sung before a charismatic healing service, we have found that we prefer to emphasize prayerful silence at Saint Luke's. When parishioners arrive the lay ministers are already there and in silent prayer. There are moments of silence throughout the service as well. Alternately, we have thought of starting with a few of the prayer and praise songs that seem most suitable for our church, plus Taizé chants such as *Jesus, Remember Me* and canons from the Episcopal hymnal. We have never done this, but we do include three hymns chosen for easy singing, familiarity, and suitability for a healing service.

When the proper time comes in the service, the celebrant invites people to come forward for the laying on of hands. We always have two ushers. One guides people to come forward and the second remains in front for anyone needing assistance to come to the altar rail. The people come first to be anointed by the celebrant and then go to one of several stations where two lay ministers of healing await them. There is usually some trepidation on the part of those coming forward and I try to catch their eyes and smile a welcome.

I have been to and participated in many services where no one has knelt, but since our services are held in a chapel with a communion rail we fell naturally into having the lay ministers stand behind the rail and the people coming for prayer kneel in front of it. We then ask people what they wish prayers for. A rather old-fashioned way of doing this is to ask, "What is your intention?" Since not many people today understand that question, I usually just ask, in a quiet, friendly fashion, "What is on your mind today?" Their answers may be anything from asking prayers for someone else to saying they are having trouble with a relationship to asking healing for cancer. I then just interiorly hand us both over to God and say, "I lay my hands on you in the name of our Lord and Savior Jesus Christ and ask...."

The words that come next are often the most difficult ones to pray. It is here that we are tempted to worry about our words being the "right" words, when what we should be doing is handing our worries to God and letting the Holy Spirit guide what we say. Here the long learning process, the year or more of trying to get ourselves out of the way and leave room for God, comes to our aid.

Some people find words learned by heart become a natural part of their prayer. Others find that words they prayed once keep coming back and are often repeated. For instance, without any planning, I found that the following prayer wrote itself in my mind and I often pray it: "May the healing love and grace of God be in every corner of your heart, crevice of your mind, and cell of your body." If someone asks prayers for someone else I always say, "We join our prayers to yours for _____ ," and include words of prayer for the person in front of me even if not asked.

All of us at Saint Luke's have found that a bit of silence following a spoken prayer gives us the best chance to pray. We end the silent prayer either very simply with "Amen" or by adding a few more words before closing.

Excellent guidelines to prayers are offered by James K. Wagner, a Methodist minister, in his book, *Blessed to be a Blessing*:

> Be brief. Long and loud prayers are unnecessary. Keep them private and personal.
>
> Be flexible. Be open to the leading of the Holy Spirit. Do not get locked into a rigid prayer formula.
>
> Be aware that the Lord of life already knows the details of the problem or situation. It is not necessary to rehearse them to him.
>
> Be intentional in your act of faith and trust, lifting up each person into the light and love of the healing Christ.[5]

◌

There are certain physical manifestations of healing that sometimes accompany healing and sometimes do not. Most of us now experience having our hands become very hot when praying for someone. But we have also come to realize that it is not necessary for our hands to become hot for healing to occur. Sometimes when we are praying for people we feel energy—like a waterfall—coursing through our hands and arms, and those we are praying for will also

---

5. James K. Wagner, *Blessed to be a Blessing* (Nashville: Upper Room, 1980), p. 57.

feel it. Sometimes we feel it and they do not. Sometimes they feel our hands as hot and *we* do not. Occasionally, when I lay hands on someone's head I feel a responding energy—like a spiritual eagerness—pulling in my prayer. At first these manifestations impressed us, but as time went on we grew to consider them of little importance.

Speaking in tongues was a part of the first Pentecost and occurred in the early church, as Paul described in his first letter to the Corinthians (14:1-19). Today in charismatic or Pentecostal services speaking in tongues often takes the form of a speaker and an interpreter. More often it is used as a prayer language. Some of us can pray in tongues but do not do so in public out of deference for those who see it as a strange custom. Since we do not teach being "slain in the Spirit" (or "resting in the Spirit") at Saint Luke's, we didn't expect it ever to happen in our services, but several times people have been touched by it. Resting in the Spirit is when, after the laying on of hands, a person is overcome by the Spirit and sinks to the floor, resting there for a short period of time. We have never had anyone fall to the floor, but we have had infrequent experiences of someone needing to stay where they were—kneeling or sitting—for a period of time, so we try to be prepared to quietly ask our partner to move over and pray for someone else while we keep the resting person company in his or her prayer.

Before ending this section it might be useful to mention two very practical details. First, in laying on hands some people press too heavily and some too lightly. I've know people who press down so strongly when laying on hands that it actually hurts! Others hover over the head, just touching the hair. Unfortunately this has the effect of a distracting tickle. What is called for is a simple laying, or placing, of the hands.

A more difficult concern is praying your spoken prayer loudly enough so that the person—who may be slightly deaf—can hear you but not so loudly as to jeopardize privacy. Leaning close helps, but if you are working in a pair your partner should also be able to hear.

∞

Whether clergy or lay, the initial call to the healing ministry often comes first to an individual. A sudden insight which keeps returning, unbidden, to the mind, or a nagging thought that will not go away is sometimes a message from the Spirit. But sometimes that call does not lead to either a liturgical ministry or a healing team.

One of the most striking examples of a special kind of healing ministry is the one at Saint Boniface Church in Sarasota, Florida, mentioned in my first chapter. A special building was built to accommodate their healing ministry, complete with several small, private rooms. People would make appointments to come. In each room they would find two people: a *channel* (the word was used long before the New Age popularized it) and an assistant who was timekeeper, witness, intercessor, and channel-in-training. The procedure was simple. They would begin by saying the Lord's Prayer together, and then the channel would lay on hands and they would pray silently together for half an hour. For this silent half-hour of prayer, the channels would have trained for four years.

Other parish healing ministries concentrate on visiting people in their homes or hospitals. Here—if approved by the clergy—a team of lay ministers visit and pray. Often the visit includes longer sessions of prayer than in a service, repeated visits, and inner healing. This type of ministry has been well described by Leo Thomas and Jean Alkire in *Healing as a Parish Ministry*.

At Saint Thomas' Episcopal Church in Cincinnati, where the late Emily Gardiner Neal once held weekly healing services, Hawley Todd leads what is called a Prayer Ministry. People desiring this ministry make appointments to come once a week for an hour for four to six weeks. Following these meetings there is an evaluation and the meetings may continue for several more months. Healing team members train for at least a year before participating and always work in pairs. Those receiving prayer must be under a doctor's or licensed therapist's care.

During the first session they explore expectations and procedures. Then—in silence—all three pray, inviting the Lord to be present. The emphasis during this period (the major part of the hour) is on listening to God. After the silence is ended, all three share what they have discerned, usually finding that it is the same, or related. When reporting on what they discerned they do not add or explain. So, for instance, if they hear "Live with me," they do not embellish on what the words might mean. The lay ministers do not usually lay hands on a person's head, although they may. There is no set method; rather, they do what seems appropriate. Often it is simply holding hands.

God's summons to an individual to be involved in the healing ministry may also be outside, or primarily outside, of a parish community. Some have become speakers and writers on healing and founders of organizations, or have led specialized ministries of inner healing, praying with the elderly, working with the sick or dying, perhaps even becoming chaplains in hospitals. One young man I met became conscious of God's healing power flowing through his hands during his work as a massage therapist, and was led to go to seminary to learn to know God better.

Since the local congregation is the main source and strength of the church, healing belongs there, but the ministry is not confined to the parish. Indeed, it is through the parish ministry that many people often hear their own specific call to a healing ministry which may or may not go beyond parish walls.

C3

A Checklist for Clergy Who Wish to Start a Healing Ministry in the Parish

1. When parishioners express an interest in a healing ministry, ask them what their understanding of healing is and how they would like to be involved. Would they be willing to study and practice for a year? Explain that you believe it should be started very carefully and under your supervision.

2. If you yourself wish to start a healing ministry, find a couple of solid, prayerful parishioners to form a committee with you. Together with them, find a few more.

3. Discuss the importance of being under the authority of the clergy as well as being accountable to one another.

4. Start by studying a book together (or begin with the biblical stories of healing and go on to a book). The first books you study should be firmly grounded in the Christian healing tradition.

5. Soon after you start reading, begin to practice laying hands on each other. Experience and practice in healing prayer and the laying on of hands are vital. Although there are important details to be learned, the primary thing is how to get yourself out of the way in order to be a channel for God's grace.

6. Teach the importance of a personal prayer life to the practice of healing.

7. Broaden your own and the group's understanding of healing by attending a variety of conferences and services. Listening to tapes can be another way to hear others speak about the ministry of healing.

8. Educate and prepare the parish for healing services before you introduce any changes to the liturgical life of the congregation.

9. Consider establishing links between your healing ministry, parish intercessions, and visiting the sick.

Inner Healing

T he summer during which I wrote the article for *Weav-ings* on the history of healing was for me a watershed period. Morning after morning I was so deeply immersed in the past that it became alive for me. When I wrenched myself out of history and into the present, I found myself becoming increasingly active in praying for a whole variety of people. But that was not all, for during the same summer I went to Bonnie Brown for inner healing for myself.

Although the emotional and circumstantial turmoil following my husband's death was now long behind me, there was still an underlying unsettledness. Grief is apt to bring other, seemingly unrelated issues to heart and mind, old griefs from childhood and unresolved issues from later years. Perhaps, I thought, inner healing would help.

In a sense, all healing is "inner healing." The Holy Spirit enters your spirit, your mind, and every cell of your body. Whatever healing comes to you is *inner.* But in the language of those active in the healing ministry today, the words "inner healing" refer to psycho-spiritual healing and in particular to what is called the *healing of memories.* These memories may be conscious and troubling ones or those forgotten memories that can cause depression and confused thinking. In short, the minister of healing who works with the healing of memories is bringing intercessory prayer to the same areas worked on by psychotherapists and their patients.

Ministers of healing working with the healing of memories usually have a good knowledge of psychological development and psychotherapy, but this knowledge is not the medicine that heals. In inner healing God is the therapist. This ministry of healing is a perfect example of getting yourself out of the way and letting the Holy Spirit use your abilities and your knowledge. Bonnie is a therapist as well as a minister of healing, but it was always very apparent that the Spirit was in charge, not Bonnie.

In a sense inner healing was not new to me that summer. I had gone to seminary many years before because I wanted to know the relationship between psychological growth in therapy and psychospiritual growth in prayer. Both within myself and within my directees I had seen and experienced the interrelatedness of psychological and spiritual growth. But in spite of my knowledge I was unprepared for the actual experience of the healing of memories.

It was the strength of the experience that surprised me. Bonnie and I would talk for awhile about my past and present and then turn to prayer. We would commit ourselves and our time together to our Lord and then center down in deep silent prayer. After awhile, Bonnie would lay on hands and we would continue in prayer. Every once in awhile she would speak to me or I to her; the words were not conversational but called forth by prayer. Bonnie would say, "Can you think of a particular time in your childhood when you felt abandoned?"

Silence would fall and I would ask the Spirit to lead my memory. Usually, after awhile a specific memory would surface.

I was ten years old and had a bad stomachache. The doctor said it was appendicitis and that my appendix should come out right away. Someone—I forget who—drove me to the hospital and I was soon tucked into a hospital bed in a private room. I felt very alone. My mother called on the phone and said that she was sorry she couldn't come to see me before the operation. Her excuse didn't make sense to me. I felt abandoned and frightened.

In the now distant present, I could hear Bonnie's voice. Her words were quiet, like one pebble dropped into a pond: "Have you remembered a time?"

"Yes."

"Do you feel as if you are there?"

"Yes, I do."

"Now invite Jesus into that place and time and see what he does." And so, silently, I asked Jesus to come into that long-ago time.

Almost immediately the door of my hospital room opened and Jesus put his head around the door. I did not feel startled, as I knew he was a friend.

"Hello, Avery. May I come in?" I nodded my head and he came over to the side of my bed. "Does your stomach hurt?"

"A bit."

"Do you miss your mother?"

"Yes. I'm scared. I wish *somebody* was here."

"I'm here," said Jesus, "and I won't leave you."

"You mean you can stay all night?"

"Yes, and tomorrow morning."

"I'm having the operation tomorrow morning."

"I know. I'll be there."

"You will? The whole time?"

"Yes, I will."

"Will you be there when I wake up?"

"Yes. I'll stay with you until you feel better."

"Thanks." I held out my hand for his.

"Do you think you can sleep now?"

"If you are here," I said, almost happily. I snuggled in the bed and closed my eyes.

In my present mind I felt a deep thankfulness and a great peace. I said to Bonnie, "It's over and I just want to pray a bit." I found myself silently and deeply caught up in loving God and I knew that Bonnie was in that place, too. How long was it? Five minutes? Twenty minutes? Eternity? Part of eternity at any rate.

Slowly I surfaced and we talked about it quietly.

✂

Such is the healing of memories. It is particularly suited to healing forgotten happenings in our lives, those in very early childhood, in infancy, in birth experiences, and in the womb. The gentle, Spirit-led words of the minister of healing may lead us back into those wordless times we thought were before memory and ask us to invite Jesus to heal them. Barbara Shlemon has described how a priest, Ted Dobson, came to her for healing of a current problem in his parish. In prayer she found herself led to pray for his infancy as an adopted child.[1] The priest was resistant to the idea but later reported:

> I began to cry. I was hearing her words from a place deep within me, a place I had never touched before. She spoke to me in the name of my natural mother and father and told me they were sorry for giving me life and then having to give me away, but it was the most loving thing they could do for me. And I forgave them. Then I spoke to my

---

1. Barbara Shlemon, *Healing the Hidden Self* (Notre Dame, Ind.: Ave Maria, 1966), pp. 63-64.

adoptive parents and told them how sorry I was for taking out on them the way I felt toward my natural mother and father, and I opened myself to the love my adoptive parents tried to give me all the years of my life.[2]

I have not often been led to pray for someone for the healing of memories, but I remember one instance at a healing conference. I was one of many asked to lay on hands during one of several services. A woman who had come to me during the first service came again and asked, "Could you pray for inner healing for me?"

The prayers at a healing service are relatively short, while the healing of memories in private practice can take an hour or longer. There would be no time to ask her about her past or present. And yet I felt called to pray for her. With people praying all around us, it was about as spiritually protected a place as I could imagine.

I laid on hands in the name of our Lord Jesus Christ and asked her to go back to a painful memory in her childhood. After a few moments of prayerful silence I asked whether she remembered such a time. She said she did and I then told her to ask Jesus into the scene and replay it in her mind.

In silent prayer I held her up to God and then asked if Jesus was there.

"Yes," she said.

Again I held her up to God in silent prayer. It was very simple and mostly silent. After a few moments I said, "Amen."

She looked up at me in wonder, tears streaming down her radiant face, and I smiled back because I knew Jesus had been with her.

---

2. Ted Dobson, *God's Great Assurance* (Ramsey, N.J.: Paulist, 1978), p. 19.

It was not until much later that I knew what had happened in any detail. In her mind she had gone back to a time when she was eight years old and her father had told her to bend over so that he could beat her with a leather belt. She was very frightened. But now when she invited Jesus into the memory he came and, sheltering her body with his, took the beating for her.

☙

Most writers on Christian healing make a point of the difference between *curing* and *healing*. Sometimes a physical cure comes with the spiritual healing and sometimes not. In my experience, when physical healing has not come while spiritual healing so clearly did, I find my faith far more fulfilled than when physical healing has occurred. In a wonderful book, *Wrestling til Dawn*, Jean Blomquist writes:

> "You're no good and you never will be!" Harsh, taunting, seething with contempt, the voice cut to my core. But I could not escape it, because the voice was my own.[3]

When the hurts of childhood have been clearly imprinted as the neglect or cruelty of others, we usually, in a sort of double vision, see them also as our fault. The inner healing needed is often neither speedy nor simple. Sins against us lead to buried anger that we suppress even further because we think anger is sinful. Yet the buried anger is more apt to lead to our own sinfulness than the anger itself, and both psychologists and ministers of healing feel that the deeper level of anger should be uncovered.

---

3. Jean M. Blomquist, *Wrestling til Dawn: Awakening to Life in Times of Struggle* (Nashville: Upper Room, 1994), p. 41.

In the same fashion, feelings of unworthiness—of being "no good"—make it difficult to be truly humble. Inner healing is a lifelong process in which the healing of memories, psychotherapy, prayer, meditation, Christian symbolism, human relationships, the direct intervention of God, and life itself may all play their parts. But one of the major actors in this healing drama is forgiveness—both being forgiven and forgiving.

Jesus laid great stress on forgiveness. "Forgive us our sins as we forgive those who sin against us," our Lord taught us to pray. "Your sins are forgiven," he said to the man lowered through the roof on a pallet by his friends. And *then* he healed him physically. In a variety of ways the leaders of the twentieth-century revival of the healing ministry have expressed the fundamental importance to healing of repentance, forgiving, and being forgiven. "What I have come to see," writes Francis MacNutt, "is how intimately the forgiveness of sins is connected with bodily and emotional healing."[4]

His wife Judith, a psychologist as well as a minister of healing, speaks often of the importance of forgiving those who have injured us before we are able to accept our healing. Emily Gardiner Neal stated that "throughout the history of the church, healing and repentance have gone hand in hand."[5] And Agnes Sanford—although raised as a Presbyterian—described at length the importance to her of preparing for and receiving the sacrament of penance in the Episcopal Church.

❦

4. Francis MacNutt, *Healing* (Altamonte Springs, Fl.: Creation House, 1988), p. 169.
5. Emily Gardiner Neal, *Celebration of Healing* (Cambridge, Mass.: Cowley Publications, 1992), p. 38.

The ministries of both inner healing and physical healing call for *discernment*. Discernment has two levels. One is
what I would call holy common sense. A wonderful example comes from John Wesley's journal:

> Reflecting today on the case of a poor woman who had
> continual pain in her stomach, I could not but remark the
> inexcusable negligence of most physicians in cases of this
> nature. They prescribe drug upon drug, without knowing a
> jot of the matter concerning the root of the disorder. And
> without knowing this, they cannot cure, though they can
> murder, the patient. Whence came this woman's pain?
> (which she would never have told, had she never been
> questioned about it)—from fretting for the death of her
> son. And what availed medicines, while that fretting con-
> tinued? Why then do not all physicians consider how far
> bodily disorders are caused or influenced by the mind; and
> in those cases, which are utterly out of their sphere, call in
> the assistance of a minister; as ministers, when they find
> the mind disordered by the body, call in the assistance of a
> physician?[6]

The other level of discernment is when the Holy Spirit
leads us to an interior knowing that we would not otherwise have. In charismatic circles this is often called receiving a *word of knowledge*. As with a gift of healing, some
people are blessed with a greater gift of discernment than
others. A remarkable example of this comes from a story
told by Jim Glennon, Canon of Saint Andrew's Cathedral
in Sydney, Australia.

A young woman called Sue was in a car accident. As far
as medical tests could ascertain, she had been uninjured in
the accident, but she suffered total amnesia. Canon Glen-

---

6. John Wesley, *The Journal of the Rev. John Wesley*, ed. Ernest Rhys
(London: J. M. Dent, n.d.), entry for May 12, 1759.

non placed his hands on her head and let the Spirit lead him in quiet prayer. He had been praying for fifteen minutes when he suddenly "saw" the accident. (He had been told nothing of it.) It was night. There were two cars. Sue was driving one. A man was in the other car that was in front of Sue's. In a spiritual discernment, or word of knowledge, Canon Glennon perceived that the man was dead. *Now* he realized why Sue had amnesia: she couldn't face the fact that she had killed a man. (Later he discovered that his vision of the accident was correct.)

What Canon Glennon did next illustrates two other aspects of inner healing. Very slowly and carefully he introduced what he had seen into his spoken prayer. He realized that *more* harm could be done by not being extremely wise and gentle in what he said. But he dared to obey the Spirit and say what the Spirit had shown him, following his words with more prayers for the healing of her memory and her ability to forgive herself. The whole process took three quarters of an hour.

At the end of the prayer there was no change in her amnesia, but over the next few weeks it rapidly dissipated and she remembered everything.[7]

Judith MacNutt recounts an experience she had as a young therapist in a mental hospital with a patient named Elizabeth: "Her hopelessness filled every corner of the room, and slowly it began to infuse my spirit too." Up until that time Judith had kept her spiritual life and her work in separate compartments, but that night she asked several friends to pray for Elizabeth.

The next morning Elizabeth was "markedly changed." She had awakened the night before at the same time they were praying. Her darkened room had been filled with

7. Jim Glennon, *Your Healing is Within You* (Plainfield, N.J.: Bridge Publications, 1978), pp. 77-81.

light and she had realized it came from Jesus. The light began to spread "warmth and healing love throughout her body and spirit." From then on her recovery was rapid.

When Judith MacNutt's patients began to get better more quickly than those treated by other therapists, she was asked what she was doing to account for this. She couldn't come up with anything unusual, and when pressed she finally said that she was praying for her patients. In return she was fired.[8]

Fortunately, the attitude of doctors has become a bit more open in recent years. Not too long ago Bonnie Brown was asked to speak by the chaplain of a nearby hospital. Though the audience was unusually small, she discovered the doctors were more interested in healing prayer than the clergy.

℈

As we became more experienced at Saint Luke's we learned something of the healing of memories, but we were primarily led in other directions. As I said earlier, inner healing takes many forms. We experienced it most profoundly in the School of Christian Healing, which came into being several years after the start of our studies.

I had felt a call to start an evening group for people who work during the day and to concentrate on healing education. I was joined by five others and we spent a wonderfully quiet year and a half studying and praying together. Then, as in the afternoon group, we offered a simple course, reading and leading a discussion of a book. At the end of eight weeks, twelve people wanted to continue with us and our numbers had grown to eighteen. We met each

---

8. Judith MacNutt, "How I Discovered Inner Healing," *Weavings*, vol. 6, no. 4 (July/August, 1991), pp. 21-22.

week, as before, to read and discuss books and—always—to end with a half hour of praying for each other.

A year later we gave a more ambitious course with outside speakers and a few of us presenting papers. This time an average of forty people a night attended! Many stayed to pray and study more with us, and the following year we repeated the course. Then an average of fifty people a night attended and, since we encouraged people to come for either single sessions or the whole course, over eighty-five people came one or more times. They did not all come from Saint Luke's, but from a wider geographical area and from many denominations. We were in awe of this bountiful harvest. What attracted the people? And what made so many of them come back for informal groups after the course was over?

Our speakers were well received, but it became obvious that it was the prayer that people wanted, the prayer and the companionship of those who were teacher/learners and to whom the healing ministry had come to be of central importance. During the year and a half that six of us met informally we learned to speak of God and to God easily and openly. We also spoke of our own inner fears and pain, and as we grew in numbers we did not lose this gift of openness.

In the early days of the twentieth century most of the people in the healing movement had great gifts. Some still do, but in a parish ministry of healing this is less apt to be the case, although God clearly helps people through our prayers. Sometimes we are asked to pray for physical healing and we do. It is rare to see an immediate physical change, but again and again people come back the following week to report, "I was amazed! Last week I felt so tense and tied up in knots and it all left! I slept like a baby that night and woke up feeling refreshed."

It is easy to tell people that you are feeling tense. It is not as easy to tell three or four people in a small group of the great ache in your heart because a relationship with your husband or wife, son, daughter, or friend has fallen apart at the seams. Nor is it easy to talk of your fears—losing your job, the operation you face, losing your mother who is dying. But when you do so and turn with hope to God and the prayers of members of the group, a slow inner transformation begins that never fails to surprise people and that keeps them coming back.

Build This House on Rock

One of the complications now facing the church and the Christian healing movement is that many Christians have turned to New Age and other non-Christian sources of healing to be healed or to learn something of healing. Just as people from mainline churches learned from the Pentecostalists and brought their learning back to their own denominations, so some Christians have learned from New Age beliefs, from healing and the mind, and from natural healing systems, and have brought what they have learned back to their churches. It seems as though the borders between non-Christian and Christian healing variously impinge, overlap, or are at odds.

New Age thinking is a large collection of beliefs and practices often influenced by Hinduism and Buddhism and usually holistic. Many charismatic Christians condemn all New Age thinking as heretical, but when holism refers to health (rather than theology) and means dealing with the whole person, it can make great sense, even though we may not agree with specific theories or treatments.

The word *holistic* is often used when describing the mind's influence on the body. Mind and body are one system. We are not so much made up of tiny bits of discrete matter as we are energy systems related to all other energy systems. A number of Christians, including some ministers of healing, have equated this universal energy with God. I have found that although I have great respect for the Christians I know who see God and this primal energy as the same thing, I believe that such thinking does Christianity a disservice. It is true that following traditional Christian theology we may speak of God as both within us and around us, but at the same time God is always *the Other*, the one to whom we pray, the One who loves us, the One whom we love.

In their emphasis on the connection between the mind and the body, many New Age philosophies are similar to those of New Thought, a movement that arose in the late nineteenth century. "New Thought" was a term that covered a wide variety of thinking and practices to do with the influence of the mind on healing.

One of the leaders of New Thought was a man with the delightful name of Phineas P. Quimby. In 1862 Mary Baker Eddy came to Quimby as a patient and was cured. She later developed her own theories and founded the Christian Science Church. Christian Science has a very different theoretical basis for healing than Christianity. In Christian Science—as in classic Hinduism—the emphasis is on pure Spirit, while sacramental understandings of Christianity affirm both matter and Spirit in Christ Jesus and in human beings.

CS

When faced with illness, Christians have always combined prayer with medicine and pastoral counseling with psychology, although sometimes prayer has been neglected in the course of treatment. In the field of medicine, the effects of one's psycho-spiritual state on one's physical well-being have long been recognized and yet more often neglected.

With the advent of X-rays, antibiotics, specialized medicine, and more and more complicated diagnostic machines, the connection between the mind and the body has often been forgotten. At the same time, scientists have been gradually proving the effect of the mind on health.

At first these proofs were more or less confined to how stress contributes to, or triggers, illness, particularly certain diseases such as arthritis and asthma. And then statistics began to prove that people whose spouses died were themselves unusually prone to develop cancer within two years. Currently, medical theory has come to believe that stress (including unresolved conflicts from childhood) opens the way for disease in general but it is our genes that predispose us to specific diseases.

It has not been until the last twenty years that interest has grown in the *positive* effect of the mind on physical illness. An unexpected leader in the field was the late Norman Cousins, who recounted the roles played by laughter and involvement in his own treatment in *Anatomy of an Illness as Perceived by the Patient*.[1] This and subsequent books raised a great deal of interest among doctors and the general public who believed that emotional and mental states influence physical healing. In *The Healer Within: The New Medicine of Mind and Body*, Dr. Steven Locke documented the history, theories, cases, and experiments that have built a foundation for this new and at the same time old branch of medicine that goes by the unwieldy name of psychoneuro-immunology (or PNI).[2]

---

1. Norman Cousins, *Anatomy of an Illness as Perceived by the Patient* (New York: Norton, 1979).
2. Steven Locke, M. D., and Douglass Colligan, *The Healer Within: The New Medicine of Mind and Body* (New York: New American Library, 1986).

Of interest to those in the healing ministry are not so much the details of the body's ability to heal itself, which are complex and only beginning to be understood, but simply the fact that the healing system exists and is affected both positively and negatively by the mind. Was it St. Augustine who said long ago, "A miracle is not contrary to nature but to what we know of nature"? Often now when I pray for someone I ask God to hurry the healing agents of the body to wherever they are needed. From time to time it becomes obvious that God does so, and that is miracle enough.

There are, of course, times when a speedier healing seems insufficient to explain a physical change. Jesus healed in many ways—by word, by touch, with a paste of spit and dust, after forgiving sins, without mentioning sin, in a crowd, at a distance—and he continues to heal in many different ways today. When I was younger I wanted explanations for everything. Now, for me, the healing that goes on in the mystery of God is cause for thanksgiving and awe and my mind is content to leave it at that.

⚬

When I was first learning about healing in our healing and prayer group at Saint Luke's following the Lenten quiet day, I was introduced to another means of healing, therapeutic touch. The theory of therapeutic touch is that we all have energy fields surrounding our bodies and that we may influence the flow of the body's energy by moving our hands slowly over a person's body (primarily touching the person's energy field, rather than his or her skin).

Therapeutic touch as a means of healing has its origins about thirty years ago in Eastern Europe. Colonel Oskar Estebany, a colonel in the Hungarian cavalry who later immigrated to Canada, had a horse to whom he was devoted. The horse became very sick and was destined to be shot in the morning. Estebany, a devout Christian, spent the whole night with his arms around the horse, praying. In the morning the horse was well. Neighbors began to ask him to pray for *their* sick animals and *they* got well. And then one day a neighbor rushed over with a sick child in his arms.

"I only pray for animals," Estebany expostulated. But the neighbor could not get the doctor and persuaded him to pray. He did so and the child got well. From then on Estebany's life was never the same. He became known as a man with a gift of healing, and his work was one of the major influences in the development of therapeutic touch some years later by Dolores Krieger.

As a nurse Dolores Krieger knew the value of touch. She and others studied Estebany's work by using Kirlian photography, which was able to show energy coming from Estebany's hands. She became convinced that such healing was not only something for gifted healers but could be learned in a secular context and taught in nursing schools. She went on to teach at New York University and has trained many others to teach.[3]

Long before I was interested in healing I went to my publisher's one day. With a puzzled expression, my editor brought out a book and, handing it to me, said, "What do you make of this?" It was a book with a title something like, "Praying for Plants." On the cover were two flats of seedlings—one prayed for and one not. The one that had been prayed for had seedlings much stronger and taller than the one that hadn't been prayed for—just like a fertilizer ad. I remember that I said, "Yes, I believe it is possi-

---

3. Dolores Krieger, *Accepting Your Power to Heal: The Personal Practice of Therapeutic Touch* (Santa Fe, N. M.: Bear & Co., 1993).

ble." And I also remember being very conscious of the inner struggle my editor was having: to him, praying for plants was obviously weird and irrational. But comparing contrasting flats of seedlings at the very least suggested scientific method. His face expressed his dilemma.

Plants entered into my own prayer life when Margaret (my spiritual directee with a gift of healing) and I decided to teach each other therapeutic touch, since this natural healing method had its start in Christian prayer and we wanted to understand it more. We found an excellent book to teach ourselves: *Therapeutic Touch: A Practical Guide* by Janet Macrae.[4] One of the suggestions in the book was to practice your sensitivity to energy fields by moving your hands very slowly over animals and plants. I am a gardener and I soon found myself practicing when I watered my garden and my house plants, and as I walked by trees, tall grass, bushes, and even hardy weeds on otherwise barren city streets. Indeed I found that I was more sensitive to the energy fields of plants than those of people. As with animals, there seemed to be no barriers.

My sensitivity to human bodies as well as to plants increased as Margaret and I practiced. She was always ahead of me but I learned. One day as she was lying on the massage table with her eyes closed, I was moving my hand very slowly a few inches over her leg. Suddenly I sensed a difference over her knee. I paused and went over it again. Margaret sensed such differences in various parts of my body all the time, but for me it was new.

After I had finished that day we talked about it. "Yes," said Margaret, "I've been having trouble with my knee." And then she said, "*I felt you pause and go back.*" Such sensitivity was beyond my imagination. Once Margaret even

4. Janet A. Macrae, *Therapeutic Touch: A Practical Guide* (New York: Alfred A. Knopf, 1987).

sensed when my hand was over one part of her body but my mind, following an inner urge, went back to concentrate on another. Such sensitivity was not mine, but with time and practice I improved.

One of the questions I have needed to confront is whether therapeutic touch is just a matter of natural healing methods, or is prayer. Would the plants in the taller of the two lots of seedlings in the contrasting flats have grown just as well through a natural human influence on energy systems without the use of prayer? Perhaps, but all healing comes from God and a great deal of unconscious or semi-conscious prayer goes on without being called prayer.

Many people learn therapeutic touch without ever thinking of prayer and some of these later realize that they are praying. Massage therapists sometimes have the same experience and nurses often find themselves called into spiritual healing. I met a seminarian once who was a massage therapist. He first realized that something was coming through his hands that had little to do with the massage techniques he had learned. Later he became conscious that God was involved in the healing process. Finally he decided to go to seminary so that he could better understand God's action in healing and train for the Christian priesthood. But many others involved in natural methods of healing may have never even thought about God's action in healing. Or they may see God in the healing but understand it in a non-Christian way. And some decide that healing is all in *their* power.

It seems to me that Christians who are praying for healing must intentionally offer themselves to Christ to use as the Spirit wishes. If the Spirit wants to use a prayer I know by heart or some other natural or learned ability of mine in the healing process, who am I to say no? We offer our whole selves to God as channels for grace.

CB

This book is about *Christian* healing. I have mentioned New Age healing, natural healing, medical, psychological, and mental healing, and therapeutic touch. How—theologically—do these relate to *Christian* healing? Is all healing Christian? Does it become Christian simply by being taught and/or done in a church? Is all healing that is not specifically Christian therefore Satanic? Are there special biblical or theological rules that define what is Christian healing and what is not? I do not pretend to know all that I should know to answer these questions, but I know enough to have formed a theological position that still needs further study and prayer.

First of all, as I indicated earlier, the witness of the New Testament is that psychological, physical, and spiritual healing comprised a large portion of Jesus' ministry on earth. The healing way of Jesus is foundationally concerned with salvation. The word *salvation* has meant many things to Christians down through the ages, from being saved from damnation to being forgiven one's sins to being freed from psychological imprisonment. But in all cases it means being close to God and being the person God created you to be.

Jesus called his disciples to pray for healing in his name. So, whatever we do as Christians, we surely should not *ignore* Christian healing; we must intentionally pray for healing in his name. When I lay on hands I always say "in the name of the Lord Jesus Christ." Other than those words I never think about what I am going to say, but I let the Spirit choose my words.

But what does it mean to pray *in his name?* We know that to Jesus doing something in someone's name meant a lot more than just a formulaic repetition of the words—although I always use them. It meant doing it in his way, according to his nature. And what was that? It was a way that was in constant communication with God. Jesus did not just rest in the fact that he *was* God, he constantly turned to God. Jesus lived in the landscape of prayer.

The New Age philosophies offer paths to God and paths to healing, but they usually base their thinking on holistic theologies, not on the incarnation of God in Christ. Of course, many things should be seen holistically. Our bodies and minds should be seen together, since clearly they interrelate. The world's ecology, economy, and society should all be seen holistically: all parts should work together. Injury to one is injury to all and blessing to one is blessing to all. Even our smallest actions or inactions affect the whole. None of these aspects of holistic thinking is incompatible with Christianity. Far from it. But when the emphasis is placed solely on the *oneness* of everything—that we are one with God—instead of the *interrelatedness* of everything—that we relate to God and God relates to us—then something central to Christian thought and practice has been lost.

In contrast to the New Age emphasis on our oneness with God, another spiritual movement popular today, Twelve Step programs, emphasize relatedness.[5] You relate to each other, to the group, to the searching demands of the Twelve Steps, and to God. If "God" is a word that makes you uncomfortable, you can relate to your "Higher Power." Twelve Step programs stress that they are spiritual and not religious, but the spiritual steps were born in the Christian context of the Oxford movement and put to-

---

5. Two books on the Twelve Steps for general Christian growth are: Terry Webb, *Tree of Renewed Life* (New York: Crossroad, 1992), and J. Keith Miller, *A Hunger for Healing* (San Francisco: Harper San Francisco, 1991).

gether with the help of Samuel Shoemaker, an Episcopal priest. In one sense no trace of Christianity remains in Twelve Step programs, but to many Christians they are wonderfully in harmony with the Christian way of relating to God, despite never mentioning Christ.

Within Christian and Jewish theology, relating to God is sometimes called relating to *the Other*. The Old Testament scholar Walter Bruggemann goes further and coins a verb to describe this way of relating: *othering*. He stresses the importance of othering in psychology, in living with neighbor and in relating to *the Other*.[6]

It seems to me that *othering* to God and neighbor is what Christian healing is all about. I do not mean in any way to reduce Christian healing to the relationship between human and human, but rather to include it, as both Moses and Jesus did: "'You shall love the Lord your God with all your heart, and with all your soul and with all your mind.'...'You shall love your neighbor as yourself'" (Matt. 22:37, 39). First and foremost, Christian healing is turning to the Other, as Jesus did in the intimacy he learned in the landscape of prayer, and—in the name of Jesus—asking help for your neighbor who is in pain.

---

6. Walter Bruggemann, "Othering With Grace and Courage," *The Anglican*, vol. 23, nos. 3 and 4 (Fall and Winter 1993-1994), pp. 11-21.

Exorcism and Deliverance

The first time that I encountered a discussion of exorcism at a healing conference I was shocked. The word *healing* brought with it connotations of hope, light, health, and joy, while the word *exorcism* conjured up a terrible battle between a priest and a soul given over to Satan. What was worse, the people at the healing conference were speaking about the occult, demons, Satanism, witchcraft, and spiritual warfare. I felt as if I had dropped into another world, and I didn't like it.

It wasn't that I didn't believe in Satan. I did and do. Long ago I'd worked out for myself a simple, practical understanding of the Prince of Evil. If Satan is a fallen angel, a fallen messenger from God, then he has no power of his own and has to ride in on God's coattails by persuading us to follow distorted views of good and God. That's why evil seems to be good to people doing evil. Like Hitler. And like me. I never *consciously* decide to be mean or cruel, but sometimes I am. A defensive way of thinking, some covering up of an old hurt, will cause me to "righteously" be selfish or mean. That, to my mind, is evil. Furthermore, Satan has a great way of hiding as a little man in a red suit and horns. The image makes us laugh, deride the idea, and decide that evil doesn't exist. Well, the little man in the red suit may not exist, but evil certainly does, and the world is full of it.

At the healing conference I was faced with new, different understandings of Satan, demons, and evil. I decided to do some reading and thinking to deepen my understanding.

I started with the Bible and various biblical reference books.[1] At one and the same time I found confusion and clarity. Consider the names of Satan: "Satan" in Hebrew (translated "the Devil" in Greek) means something between adversary, accuser, and slanderer, and there is no single, accurate English equivalent. Satan is also given a whole range of other titles, such as *prince of demons, dragon, ancient serpent, god of this world, ruler of this world, tempter, Beelzebul* or *Beelzebub*, and simply *enemy*.

But the name *Lucifer* receives the crown of confusion. In Latin it means "light bearer" and in classical mythology that word is used for Venus. Venus is the Daystar. Isaiah 14:12 in the King James Version reads: "How art thou fallen from heaven, O Lucifer, son of the morning!" The Vulgate, Jerome, and the church fathers speak of Satan as Lucifer, but most modern Bibles translate Lucifer as "Daystar." To make matters worse, *Day-star* is a term also used for Christ (2 Peter 1:19 and Revelation 2:28). Although many translations now say "morning star," the familiar hymn *Christ, Whose Glory Fills the Skies* asks: "Day-spring from on high, be near; Day-star, in my heart appear." Hoping to throw further light on the subject, I looked up "Lucifer" in the multi-volume *Anchor Bible Dictionary*, but since the word was no longer in the Bible it was not listed.

The Old Testament mentions Satan relatively little, but during the intertestamental period Israel's perceptions of the Prince of Darkness matured. Satan is mentioned thirty-five times in the New Testament and there is no

---

1. Chiefly the *Anchor Bible Dictionary* (Doubleday, 1992), particularly the article on the devil by Duane Watson in vol. 2, pp. 183-184 and the article on Satan by Victor Hamilton in vol. 5, pp. 985-989.

doubt that Jesus believed in the reality and power of Satan. In a concluding summary paragraph to her book, *The Demise of the Devil*, Susan Garrett writes:

> The ministry of Jesus is from its inception a struggle with Satan for authority. At the testing in the wilderness Satan tries to divert Jesus from his God-appointed task by persuading him, too, to worship Satan as Lord. When Jesus by his obedience to God resists the devil's power, the devil departs, defeated. But Jesus' final victory is not yet won: Satan will continue to oppose him throughout Jesus' earthly ministry, and will regain authority at the passion. For a brief period it looks as if the devil has conquered Jesus: darkness settles over the face of the earth, and Jesus dies. But then Jesus is exalted to the place at the right hand of God, and Satan falls from heaven. Henceforth (as during Jesus' ministry prior to the passion) all the faithful who call upon the name of the Lord will have authority over the Enemy's power. Their own names are written with Christ in heaven.[2]

How one names the prince of demons, and how one translates those names, pales in significance before the story as a whole. For Jesus, Satan was far from being a minor matter of semantics. Fighting the power of Satan was a major concern—if not *the* major concern—of Jesus' life and ministry.

The most complete statement about Satan in the scriptures occurs in the Revelation to John:

> And war broke out in heaven; Michael and his angels fought against the dragon. The dragon and his angels fought back, but they were defeated, and there was no

---

2. Susan R. Garrett, *The Demise of the Devil* (Minneapolis: Augsburg/Fortress, 1989).

longer any place for them in heaven. The great dragon was thrown down, that ancient serpent, who is called the Devil and Satan, the deceiver of the whole world—he was thrown down to the earth, and his angels were thrown down with him.

Then I heard a loud voice in heaven, proclaiming, "Now have come the salvation and the power and the kingdom of our God and the authority of his Messiah, for the accuser of our comrades has been thrown down, who accuses them day and night before our God. But they have conquered him by the blood of the Lamb and by the word of their testimony, for they did not cling to life even in the face of death. Rejoice then, you heavens and those who dwell in them! But woe to the earth and the sea, for the devil has come down to you with great wrath, because he knows that his time is short!" (Revelation 12:7-12)

More of the prophetic poetry of Revelation follows and Satan is thrown into the bottomless pit for one thousand years, let out for awhile, and then defeated forever. The final victory of the Messiah is described in words of awesome beauty in the twenty-first chapter of the Book of Revelation.

It is tempting to try to figure out the timetable of John's vision, but that is a sidetrack that has left many waiting on a mountain top and I have no desire to follow them. What is apparent among Christians today, as it was in the time of the New Testament, is that battling with Satan is a part of our lives. Within each of us Jesus' victory over Satan comes, comes again, and will come yet again. Jesus' gift of salvation is complete but our acceptance of it is far from complete. It is in that lack of completion that Satan has room to act and we to respond. Insofar as we are open to healing, Jesus' battle with and victory over Satan comes within each of us—not once but many times.

In the gospels the casting out of demons was part of Jesus' fight against Satan. His attitude toward it was very matter-of-fact: when he saw the need, he cast them out. As Walter Wink says:

> In his encounter with the demonic there was no protracted struggle, no violence aimed at the exorcist, no magical words, crucifixes, holy water—not even the invocation of the divine name. Jesus is totally calm, totally in control. There is no question, as in certain healings (Mark 8:22-26; 6:1-6), whether Jesus will prevail. The demons are depicted as weak fractions of power unable to tolerate the presence of divine authority.[3]

In both the Bible and the early church, exorcism—the casting out of demons—was seen to be a type of healing, but was treated somewhat differently. In anointing and the laying on of hands, Jesus Christ's healing power was asked to come into a person and make him or her well. In exorcism, the exorcist *commands* in the name of Jesus that demons, or evil spirits, leave the person.

In the early church some Christians, both lay and clergy, seemed more naturally suited to do exorcisms than others. Soon a growing number of people were called *exorcists.* By the middle of the third century, exorcists were ordained to a special minor order. It was a period of many strange spiritual allegiances, and these had to be disavowed if a person wanted to become a Christian. The exorcists spent much of their time employed in exorcising those in the catechumenate and candidates for baptism. It was a simple and orderly way of getting rid of the wrong spiritual baggage, and it was done quite routinely. In time this minor

---

3. Walter Wink, *Unmasking the Powers: The Invisible Forces That Determine Human Existence* (Philadelphia: Fortress, 1986), p. 58.

order ceased as the pagan world gave way to the Christian world, and it was absorbed into the priesthood.[4]

The view of exorcism in the Bible and the early church seemed very far removed from either my enculturated image of a priest struggling with a totally possessed person or the workshop on deliverance and exorcism that had shocked me so at the healing conference. Yet the more I read about healing, the more people in the healing ministry I heard and came to know, and the more I prayed for people, the more I began to realize that I could not just dismiss the subject of exorcism as having nothing to do with me. It was part of healing. And so I continued to read and pray.

⍥

My first personal experience came when I was meeting with Bonnie Brown for inner healing. After we had worked together for a good number of weeks and she had grown to know me well, she took me by surprise one day.

"Avery," she said, "I have become convinced that there was something evil about your mother and I'd like to suggest that you do a compassionate exorcism."

Now by that time my mother had been dead for over forty years, so Bonnie was not suggesting a personal confrontation in the usual sense. We had never spoken about my mother as being troubled by evil spirits, but the idea made sense to me. Demons often enter a crack opened by childhood trauma. My mother had had such a trauma and so had *her* mother, my grandmother. My grandmother's mother died when my grandmother was a little girl and she grew up to be a cool and distant woman. I cannot imagine

---

4. P. J. Toner, article in *The Catholic Encyclopedia*, vol. 5 (New York: Robert Appleton, 1909), pp. 709-711.

her being warm to my mother. Then, when my mother was
a little girl, her father died of typhoid fever. And there, in
three generations, were cracks for evil spirits. I might call
them neuroses, but one could certainly see them as evil
spirits and suddenly I saw them in that way. They were not
evil spirits calling for elaborate rites by priests appointed
by the bishop. They were evil spirits that needed to be cast
out by a daughter who felt compassionate about and
lonely for her long dead mother.

Bonnie and I centered down in deep, silent prayer and
then she said quietly, "Imagine your mother at any time
you wish."

I did not search my mind but waited for the Lord's leading and in a few moments I saw myself standing by my
mother's bed as she lay dying. I spoke to her quietly about
my realizing how hard it had been for her to be brought up
by a mother who knew nothing of mothering and then to
have her father die. And then—still in my mind—I said
very simple words of exorcism: "In the name of the Lord
Jesus Christ I bind all evil spirits that trouble you and send
them to you, Lord, for you to do with as you will."

As soon as I spoke the words my interior memory
changed radically. A pillar of light streamed down over my
mother and me. The whole atmosphere changed. The room
had been grey and hopeless. Now joy sang in the air and
permeated my very being.

How long do such spiritual experiences last? A minute?
An hour? Eternity. I know that I didn't want it to end but
knew I should leave. Slowly I returned to the present.
From that day on my memory of my mother has been of
the young woman she never was—free, happy, content, and
my companion in both past and present.

It was not long after my experience of exorcising my
mother that I was laying on hands and praying in a small

healing prayer group. As is my usual practice, after I had spoken words of prayer I continued praying silently and contemplatively. When quietly open to the Spirit in this way, words and images sometimes come unexpectedly to mind. This time what came was an image of darkness. Instinctively I reacted with silent words of exorcism. When I later said, "Amen," the person I had been praying for looked at me in wonder and said, "While you were praying I'd been distracted by invasive black images and then suddenly, they all flew away."

These two experiences had seemed natural and right to me but it was nonetheless good to read in a scholarly article by Robert Faricy, SJ, that what I was doing was called a *private exorcism*, which is usually done silently and has a long tradition of lay as well as clergy use.[5]

Cʒ

Most charismatics would use the word *deliverance* to describe the private exorcisms I have been describing. *Deliverance*, according to Francis MacNutt, is "a process, mainly through prayer, of freeing a person who is *oppressed* by evil spirits." He describes *exorcism* as "a formal ecclesiastical prayer to free a person possessed by evil spirits."[6]

Both the Roman Catholic and Episcopal churches say that the Rite of Exorcism may only be done by bishops or their appointees. But, as the early church recognized, there is a need for a vast range of spiritual practices, all referring to the casting out of evil spirits. In practice, exorcism is re-

---

5. Robert Faricy, SJ, "Deliverance from Evil: Private Exorcism," in *Deliverance Prayer*, ed. Matthew and Dennis Linn (New York/Ramsey: Paulist Press, 1981), pp. 72-85.
6. Francis MacNutt, *Healing* (Altamonte Springs, Fl.: Creation House, 1988), p. 215.

ally a continuum between such minor exorcisms as I have described and the major Rite of Exorcism. As one approaches the use of the major rite, the need for greater discernment and extreme caution increases markedly. No casting out of evil spirits, even the most minor, should be approached lightly.

In a little book called *Satan Stalking*, the author who has long been troubled by dark spirits, describes her experience of deliverance in a healing service at a Cursillo:

> I thought, "God is here, I should ask for healing."...The priest leaned close, and I whispered..."I need to be delivered from an evil spirit, or some evil spirits." He didn't seem shocked. I knelt in front of him and he held my hand with one hand, and put the other on my head....I was knocked down with a delightful force, like electric butterflies coursing all through my body. I couldn't move, overwhelmed by the powerful and wonderful feeling. I was being cleaned from the inside, head to toe. The beautiful, dancing, living water washed every cell, and I was filled with light.[7]

And she was indeed delivered from crippling fears and darkness that had been troubling her all her life.

Among charismatics, deliverance ministry has become a specialized ministry within the healing ministry. It is often combined with inner healing and employs a whole range of aids to deliver people from the power of evil spirits. Chief among these is healing prayer itself, but pastoral counseling, psychotherapy, and medical treatment all play their part.

Much of the deliverance ministry concentrates on psychological problems. Were many of the demons and evil spirits cast out in the Bible and the early church really

7. Dorothy Marie England, *Satan Stalking* (Cincinnati: Forward Movement Publications, 1993), p. 52.

what we call neuroses and mental illness? It would certainly seem so when we hear the words of Origen, the great third-century theologian: "By invoking the name of Jesus, we have seen many persons freed from grievous calamities and from distractions of mind and madness and countless other ills." This makes very modern sense of the fact that exorcism is both routine and yet sometimes major. We are *all* neurotic, we *all* have distorted ideas of ourselves and the world, and we *all* need to get rid of demons.

The part of deliverance ministry that made me uncomfortable when I attended the workshop a good number of years ago was dealing with the occult, including witchcraft, Satanism, astrology, and fortune telling. It still makes me uncomfortable, but I no longer think that deliverance from the occult belongs only to the Middle Ages. How widespread serious occult activities, such as Satanism and witchcraft, are is a matter of controversy, but they clearly exist. How serious minor occult activities, such as casual fortune telling, are is also a matter of controversy. I tend to believe that they are much less serious than most charismatics believe, but I do think they are rather like crossing the street against a red light. The risk is there.

According to the British Christian Exorcism Study Group, which put together the excellent book *Deliverance: Psychic Disturbances and Occult Involvement*, the most frequent occult problems are occasioned by poltergeists or ghosts.[8] The book provides clear instructions for the investigation of such disturbances, and directions for follow-up practices. A house blessing and/or house exorcism is often useful, but should not be seen as a magic rite; rather it is

---

8. Michael Perry, ed., *Deliverance: Psychic Disturbances and Occult Involvement* (London: SPCK, 1987), p. 12. Distributed in the U.S. by the United Methodist Publishing House.

part of integrating all members of the household more deeply into the Christian faith.

⚬

From the early days of the church, certain people have been seen as better suited to cast out demons than others. This is also true of the deliverance ministry today. Two characteristics seem to predominate. The first is a simple, strong, and uncomplicated faith. The second is the ability to speak with quiet authority based on that faith. Those casting out demons must not be ashamed to confess their faith in Christ crucified and must not waver, but speak firmly and with confidence.

For many years we had a handyman who gave us a few hours of his time each week. Charlie is a wonderful Christian. He is a Baptist and some of our ways of speaking about our lives in Christ are different, while others are wonderfully the same. We often prayed together and became spiritual friends. Once, when I was preparing a talk for my group on healing in the Annand Program at Yale, Charlie asked what I was doing. "I'm preparing a talk on exorcism and deliverance, Charlie," I responded.

There was a pause and then Charlie, with a quiet smile, replied, "I only know the Good One."

To remain centered on Jesus Christ, "the Good One," is essential in any prayers of deliverance or exorcism. Traditionally words of exorcism—and deliverance as a lesser form—are *commands*. You aren't petitioning God, you are, in the name of Jesus, commanding evil spirits to leave. To say words of exorcism or deliverance is an act of faith in Jesus Christ. Moreover, it is an act of faith in the grace and power we have been given by being Christian, by being part of Christ's church.

I always begin words of deliverance, as is traditional, with "In the name of the Lord Jesus Christ," but then I usually add, "and by the authority committed unto me by my baptism." Whether I say it or not, it is the only authority I have. To stand up to evil spirits clothed only in my own humanity is to invite disaster. I always follow these words by a "binding prayer."

A binding prayer is a bridge between prayer and exorcism and may be either. The purpose is to bind the evil spirits from activity. I usually say one silently before a meeting for healing. It puts us all under the protection of Christ and reminds me that we are under that protection. Here is an example:

Binding Prayer Before a Meeting
(usually done silently or with the leaders)

Lord Jesus Christ, in your name I [we] ask protection for this building [home, room] and all of us in it. Bind any evil spirits that might wish us ill so that they are incapable of hurting anyone. Protect us from harm through the day and through the night. Amen.

Another binding prayer moves across the bridge of prayer into minor exorcism. It is essentially the same prayer I prayed for my mother and I often use it silently when praying for people.

Binding Prayer for an Individual

In the name of the Lord Jesus Christ I bind all evil spirits that would assault [Name] from within or without and send them to you, Lord, to do with as you wish.

I follow it with such prayers of protection and healing as I am moved to pray.

Petra, a member of our healing group at Saint Luke's who moved to Philadelphia, wrote to me one day to tell me of a time she had need of this binding prayer.

> In the middle of the evening our friend's three-year-old child, who had been asleep for an hour or so, began to flail about in his bed, wildly knocking his head against the wall and groaning loudly and incoherently. I was alarmed, but the parents told me that he was having a night terror and the doctors had told them there was nothing they could do. I discreetly went into an empty room adjacent to the child's and offered a prayer that came out as a binding prayer, thanks to your gentle introduction. Before I had finished praying, it was completely silent in the next room. The night terror had vanished and he was sleeping peacefully. So, as always, who knows? I certainly don't, but the coincidence is striking.

C8

Many Protestants are freer of prohibitions against exorcism than Episcopalians and Roman Catholics, and they see many paths to casting out evil spirits. After the summer we spent praying for my inner healing, Bonnie and I began to meet simply to pray for each other. One day she said to me that she needed to work something out with Christ. She didn't tell me what but just said that she would like my silent prayer as she did so. I agreed and we centered down in deep contemplation. I simply concentrated on Christ and on lifting Bonnie up to Christ. It was contemplative intercession.

About thirty minutes into the silence I was conscious of Bonnie saying something. Her voice was different—deep, guttural, and hard to understand. I made out some words about control. I remained in silence, and with confidence in the power and protection of Jesus Christ I lifted her in prayer again. Later I asked Bonnie, "Was that mostly about giving control to God?"

"Yes," she said, "it was. I was asking deliverance from the desire to be in control rather than letting God be in control."

A more frightening brush with an evil spirit came one time when Irene and I were in another city doing a conference. After the conference we visited an old friend of mine for lunch. A Methodist clergyman, he and I had become frequent prayer partners at healing conferences. After lunch he led us into his study and closed the door.

"I've been having some trouble," he said, "and when I knew the two of you were coming I decided to ask you a big favor. My wife, as you know, had two children by her first husband. They were almost grown when we married and they've been out of college and on their own for some time. Her son has had various problems for years. We've done what we could but that's not much. Recently he came home for what he said was a short visit but it has gone on for two months now. He's always welcome here but what has not been welcome has been his behavior. He's been manipulative and divisive. He deliberately sets me against my wife and my wife against me. I've become convinced that he's being troubled by an evil spirit."

Turning to me he said, "Avery, will you—with our support—do a quiet exorcism?"

"He is at home?" I asked.

"Yes, but I wasn't thinking of his being in the room with us."

I thought for a moment. With my two praying friends, one of them clergy, we could not be more spiritually protected. So I said yes and the three of us centered down in prayer. We were seated and after a few minutes we laid our hands one on top of the other. After a few more minutes of silent prayer I said a binding prayer and, in the name of Jesus Christ, cast out the demon.

Immediately I felt an electric shock go up my right hand and arm. It did not feel evil but more like God telling me that something had happened. My arm felt the results of the shock for the rest of the day. The next morning the young man left town. He came back two years later for another visit. He was cheerful, agreeable, and an agent for family peace. I thanked God—but was also grateful that I did not believe I was being called into the deliverance ministry.

A year or so earlier I had written to my bishop asking if there was an official Episcopal exorcist in the diocese. I had asked because in my class in healing in the Annand Program I gave a session on exorcism and deliverance, and I wanted to be able to tell the Episcopal students whether an exorcist was readily available or not. The bishop replied that there was no official exorcist in the diocese. A year after my inquiry I received a call from the rector of an Episcopal church saying that he was calling because the bishop had told him to. The priest had someone who might need an exorcism in his parish and the bishop had suggested he call me for advice. I was dumbfounded! And yet I had become convinced that the British system of having advisors in each diocese and having the parish priest do such minor exorcism as was needed was holy common sense. If I was the best "expert" available, then so be it. I said that I would help in any way I could.

A year after that the bishop's office in a neighboring diocese called me in to consult. I had a long interview with the person they were concerned about, said some healing prayers, and concluded that no exorcism was needed. Nevertheless, I was haunted by the specter of becoming widely known as a consultant and suggested that they raise up and train their own advisors.

Around this time I read a book called *Hostage to the Devil* by Malachi Martin describing formal major exorcisms of the kind that fascinate the public and frighten anyone with a grain of sense.[9] These are the kind of exorcisms that make it very sensible to say that only a bishop or the bishop's appointee should do them. But how do we know the difference? Mostly, I believe, by a combination of common sense and prayerful discernment. If I were a priest and a person came to me complaining of demons, I would make an appointment for a lengthy interview and do some hearty praying before the interview. I would say a silent binding prayer immediately beforehand and open the interview with a simple prayer for guidance.

As I talked with the person I would consider whether he or she seemed to me to be relatively well-balanced emotionally other than the presenting symptoms. I would ask whether there were any psychological problems. I would inquire whether the person was taking any medications and, if so, what they were. Many medications have side-effects that may be confused with demonic possession, and a schizophrenic has symptoms of hearing voices. I may want to get permission to speak to his or her doctor or therapist or suggest an evaluation if the person is not under a doctor's or therapist's care. (This does not mean that I would summarily dismiss a possible satanic origin for the problem.) I would ask if he or she had had any involvement with the occult, either as a child or an adult. My questions on all subjects would be thorough but very gentle and non-condemnatory.

---

9. Malachi Martin, *Hostage to the Devil* (New York: Readers Digest Press, 1976).

Then I would inquire about spiritual practices. Does he or she go to church regularly? Pray at home? Read the Bible? One's own prayers, as well as those of others, are the major weapons against Satan. The confession of sin, either sacramentally or more informally, is a major aid, and all the sacraments help.

Finally, I would offer prayers of healing, with or without the laying on of hands. If possible, I would like to have someone experienced in the healing ministry with us in the interview to help me discern. Certainly I would want that person with us for the healing prayers, which I would like to do in the church.

All of the above would usually take more than one meeting. I would keep reminding myself that what I should be primarily interested in is the person's spiritual health. If the person has a healthy relationship with God and neighbor and has done everything else available to fight the presenting problem, then he or she may well need deliverance ministry. If it looked and felt serious to me, then I would call my bishop.

The complete surrender to Satan is as rare as the complete surrender to God of a great saint. Still, in between the need for major exorcism and the need for healing prayer is the whole field of deliverance and private and minor exorcism. In today's world, fear of the very word "exorcism" surely should not keep any Christian from rebuking Satan and performing private, silent exorcisms and simple deliverances. As with Christian healing, so with Christian exorcism: it is not a matter of magic rites but of stepping out in faith in the power of Jesus Christ.

The deliverance ministry can do great work but it can also get out of hand, as charismatic Protestants involved in that ministry readily admit.[10] Perhaps the time has come for the revival of the minor order of exorcists, which would give the church the opportunity to train those gifted in this area and to ensure that their ministry of exorcism is grounded in a deep involvement with prayer.

10. John and Mark Sandford, *Deliverance and Inner Healing* (Grand Rapids, Mich.: Chosen Books, 1992), see particularly p. 26.

Healing the World

This epilogue has an audacious, even arrogant, title. What can I say about healing the world—a subject so large it is hard even to imagine? And insofar as healing and salvation are one, Christ has already saved the world. Yet unless we cooperate with God, unless we accept salvation, the world will not be healed. Let me narrow the subject. I'm not proposing to say anything specific about theology, politics, or ecology, but only to speak about prayer. What part may prayer play in the healing of the world?

What I have said in this book has been primarily addressed to individuals interested in understanding and furthering the healing ministry in local parishes. But it is not just a few individuals who need healing: it is the church, our country, our civilization, and the world. All of them seem to be slipping and sliding toward some unknown but disastrous destiny, helped out by evil forces which are seemingly beyond our control or influence. In writing this book I've often been visited by thoughts of these larger issues. What does my subject, healing in the landscape of prayer, have to offer to us as we face these vast and depressing prospects?

Walter Wink speaks powerfully of the importance of intercessory prayer in the healing of the world:

> History belongs to the intercessors, who believe the future into being. This is not simply a religious statement. It is as true of communists or capitalists or anarchists as it is of Christians. The future belongs to whoever can envision in

the manifold of its potentials a new and desirable possibility, which faith then fixes upon as inevitable. This is the politics of hope. Hope envisages its future and then acts as if that future is now irresistible, thus helping to create the reality for which it longs.[1]

Prayer calls for and offers hope. Hope is a neglected virtue today. It is both fashionable and deadly to despair. Yet without hope we will fail. And the lack of hope has eroded faith. It isn't only that we despair of *our* being able to solve the vast problems we face, we despair of *God* being able to solve them. God has become for many merely a symbol and no longer really God. Theologically we may argue about how much of our Creator's omnipotence God has given up to allow us freedom, but surely God hasn't given up *all* power.

The lack of hope has also eroded love. We pray for our friends but seldom for our enemies. It's all too much for us. We give up. We dismiss the world's terrible problems from our minds and hearts—with or without a passing prayer—as rapidly as possible. Thoughts of the world's sufferings are painful and too heavy for us to bear. We vent our fears by getting angry at those "stupid" or "evil" people who we believe are causing part or all of the problem.

How can we bear to pray for all the horrors of the world? The Quakers have a tradition of having "a concern," usually seen as an area of good works. They believe that God gives each of us one particular concern: to work for peace, or with the blind, the elderly, the homeless, children, and so forth. Not for *all* the troubles in the world,

---

1. Reprinted from *Engaging the Powers: Discernment and Resistance in a World of Domination*, page 299, by Walter Wink, © 1992, by permission of Augsburg/Fortress.

but just for that one concern to which God is calling someone. As in good works, so in prayer.

Some of us may be called to pray for all the pain and
problems of the world, as in the old Hasidic tale in which
God says that he hasn't destroyed the world because of the
insistent prayers of a poor widow. But if praying for the
whole world seems overwhelming to you, then ask God
what specific problem you are called to pray for. I find that
I can bear to look deeply at one large and terrible dilemma
and hold it up to God in prayer. Opening myself in this
way to the despair of one problem I may—with good con-
science—say of the others, "They are too much for me,
Lord. With gratitude I leave them to you."

Agnes Sanford, in her later years, bought a house in
California directly on the San Andreas Fault. Undaunted,
she decided to pray for the healing of the earth beneath
her. Sometimes our prayer concerns, whether personal or
global, are given to us in just such a clear and immediate
fashion. While writing this book I found myself almost
driven to pray for the church. In learning about healing I
have gained a great deal from charismatic evangelicals, but
they are all too often scorned or ignored by liberals and
academicians. On the other hand, many charismatic evangelicals choose to scorn or ignore liberals and academicians. Somewhere in the middle I pray for all sides, not so
much that they will change their minds but that they may
find in the other what they can admire and thank God for.
For the most part, when I pray for Christ's church I do so
in wordless intercession. With all its divisions, failures,
weakness, stupidities, and heresies unspecified, I simply
hold the church up to God.

There is another way in which prayer may help to heal
the world. I speak now not about healing prayer specifically but about the landscape of prayer—that deep opening

to the Spirit which not only gives us an interior vision but influences how we see our exterior world. It is the Spirit of God who can lead us to see new ways of understanding the church, world, and civilization that are both tied to our traditions and open to the future.

I acknowledge with gratitude the help of William Doubleday and Bonita Palmer in updating the following:

Suggestions for Further Reading

∞ *Healing in History*

- Cox, Harvey. *Fire from Heaven: The Rise of Pentecostal Spirituality and the Reshaping of Religion in the Twenty-first Century.* Reading, Massachusetts: Addison Wesley, 1995. (A thought-provoking study.)
- Daniels, W. H., ed. *Dr. Cullis and His Work: Twenty Years of Blessing in Answer to Prayer.* Boston: Willard Tract Repository, 1885. Facsimile edition, part of Higher Christian Life Series. Garland, 1985.
- DeArteaga, William. *Quenching the Spirit.* Altamonte Springs, Florida: Creation House, 1992. (From a Protestant point of view.)
- Kelsey, Morton T. *Healing and Christianity: A Classic Study.* Revised edition. Minneapolis: Augsburg/Fortress, 1994.
- Remus, Harold. *Jesus as Healer.* Cambridge: Cambridge University, 1997.
- Smith, David H. *Health and Medicine in the Anglican Tradition.* New York: Crossroad, 1986. (Excellent theological and ethical exploration.)

◌Ʒ *Healing in the Parish*

- Alkire, Jan. *Healing Stories of Faith, Hope and Love.* New York and Mahwah, New Jersey: Paulist Press, 2003. (An excellent new book.)
- Bullitt-Jonas, Margaret. *Holy Hunger.* New York: Knopf, 1999. (A personal spiritual reflection on eating disorders by an Episcopal priest.)
- Cohen, Cynthia, et al. *Faithful Living, Faithful Dying: Anglican Reflections on the End of Life.* Harrisburg, Pennsylvania: Morehouse Publishing, 2000.
- Dudley, Martin, and Geoffrey Rowell, editors. *The Oil of Gladness: Anointing in the Christian Traditions.* London: SPCK, 1995.
- Evans, Abigail Rian. *Redeeming Marketplace Medicine: A Theology of Health Care.* Cleveland, Ohio: Pilgrim Press, 1999. (A superb reflection on contemporary medicine and the need for the Church to play a role.)
- Heinz, Donald. *The Last Passage: Recovering a Death of Our Own.* Oxford: Oxford University Press, 1998. (A fine reflection on end of life issues by an ordained Lutheran.)
- Heron, Benedict M., OSB. *Channels of Healing Prayer.* Notre Dame, Indiana: Ave Maria Press, 1992.
- MacNutt, Francis. *Healing in the Parish.* Notre Dame, Indiana: Ave Maria Press, 1999. (The bestselling classic, revised and expanded.)
- Maddocks, Morris. *The Christian Healing Ministry: New Edition.* London: SPCK, 1995. (A revised volume by a distinguished Anglican bishop who has been a leader in healing ministry.)

- Miller, J. Keith. *A Hunger for Healing: The Twelve Steps as a Classic Model for Christian Spiritual Growth.* San Francisco: HarperSanFrancisco, 1991.
- Mumford, Nigel. *Hand to Hand: From Combat to Healing.* New York: Church Publishing Company, 2000.
- Neal, Emily Gardiner, edited by Anne Cassel. *The Reluctant Healer.* Revised edition. Colorado Springs, Colorado: Waterbrook Press, a division of Random House, 2000. Original title: *Celebration of Healing.* Boston, MA: Cowley Publications, 1992.
- Norberg, Tilda, and Robert D. Webber. *Stretch Out Your Hand: Exploring Healing Prayer.* Nashville: Upper Room, 1998.
- ———. *Stretch Out Your Hand: Exploring Healing Prayer; A Leader's Guide.* Nashville: Upper Room, 1998.
- Pattison, Stephen. *Alive and Kicking: Towards a Practical Theology of Illness and Healing.* Harrisburg, Pennsylvania: SCM/Trinity Press International (a division of Morehouse), 1989.
- Paulsell, Stephanie. *Honoring the Body: Meditations on a Christian Practice.* San Francisco: Jossey-Bass, 2002. (A moving reflection on the reverent care of one's own body as a spiritual practice in the pursuit of health and holiness.)
- Plater, Ormond. *Intercession: A Theological and Practical Guide.* Boston: Cowley, 1995. (Mostly for church services, but useful for all who pray for others.)
- Shlemon, Barbara Leahy, Dennis Linn, SJ, and Matthew Linn, SJ. *To Heal as Jesus Healed.* Notre Dame, Indiana: Ave Maria Press, 1992.
- Thomas, Leo, OP, and Jan Alkire. *Healing Ministry: A Practical Guide.* Kansas City, Missouri: Sheed & Ward, 1994.

- ————. *Healing as a Parish Ministry.* Notre Dame, Indiana: Ave Maria Press, 1992.

○§ *A Life of Prayer*

Useful books for an introductory study of prayer include:

- Anonymous. *The Way of a Pilgrim.* Trans. Reginald M. French. San Francisco: HarperSanFrancisco, 1984. (The classic on the Jesus Prayer.)
- Barry, William, SJ. *Discernment in Prayer: Paying Attention to God.* Notre Dame, Indiana: Ave Maria Press, 1990.
- Benson, Robert. *Living Prayer.* New York: Tarcher/Putnam, 1998.
- Brooke, Avery. *Finding God in the World.* Boston: Cowley Publications, 1993. Out of print; author has copies for $10 each. 27 Pasture Lane, Noroton, CT, 06820. (A spiritual autobiography that covers a good deal about learning to pray.)
- Bruggeman, Walter. *Praying the Psalms.* Revised edition. Winona, Minnesota: St. Mary's Press, 1993. (My favorite book about the psalms.)
- Collins, Pat, CM. *Prayer in Practice.* Maryknoll, New York: Orbis Books, 2001.
- de Mello, Anthony. *Sadhana, a Way to God: Christian Exercises in Eastern Form.* Garden City, NY: Image/Doubleday, 1984. (A short book packed with descriptions of forty-seven exercises in prayer and meditation.)
- Foster, Richard J. *Celebration of Discipline: The Path to Spiritual Growth.* San Francisco: HarperSanFrancisco, 1978. (This popular Quaker author describes traditional spiritual disciplines.)

- Guenther, Margaret. *The Practice of Prayer*. Boston: Cowley Publications, 1998. (A modern classic.)
- Hall, Thelma. *Too Deep for Words*. Mahwah, NJ: Paulist, 1988. (Lectio divina.)
- Keating, Thomas. *The Better Part: Stages of Contemplative Living*. New York: Continuum, 2000.
- Brother Lawrence. *The Practice of the Presence of God*. Grand Rapids, Michigan: Fleming H. Revell Co., reissue edition, 1999. (A short, classic book on how to pray in the midst of life. By a seventeenth-century lay brother.)
- Merton, Thomas. *Contemplative Prayer*. New York: Image Books, Doubleday, reissue edition, 1971. (More advanced.)
- ———. *New Seeds of Contemplation*. New York: New Directions, 1961. (Books by and about Thomas Merton abound. This is one of the best and most useful.)
- Quoist, Michel; translated by Elizabeth Lovatt-Dolan. *New Prayers*. New York: Herder & Herder, 1990.
- Smith, Martin L., SSJE. *The Word is Very Near You: A Guide to Praying with Scripture*. Cambridge, Mass.: Cowley Publications, 1989. (A superbly useful book.)
- Underhill, Evelyn. *Mysticism: A Study in the Nature and Development of Man's Spiritual Consciousness*. New York: Doubleday, 1990. (A classic book about the writings of saints and mystics. Not for beginners.)

ෆ෫ *Inner Healing*

- Augsburger, David. *Helping People Forgive*. Louisville, Kentucky: Westminster John Knox Press, 1996. (An exploration of the spiritual and psychological dynamics of forgiveness.)

- Blomquist, Jean M. *Wrestling til Dawn: Awakening to Life in Times of Struggle.* Nashville: Upper Room, 1994.
- Droege, Thomas A. *The Healing Presence: Spiritual Exercises for Healing, Wellness and Recovery.* San Francisco: HarperSanFrancisco, 1992.
- Linn, Dennis and Matthew Linn. *Healing Life's Hurts: Healing Memories Through Five Stages of Forgiveness.* New York: Paulist, 1978.
- Miller, J. Keith. *A Hunger for Healing: The Twelve Steps as a Classic Model for Christian Spiritual Growth.* San Francisco: HarperSanFrancisco, 1991.
- Sandford, John Loren, and Mark Sandford. *Deliverance and Inner Healing.* Grand Rapids, Michigan: Chosen Books, 1992.
- Shlemon, Barbara. *Healing the Hidden Self.* Notre Dame, Indiana: Ave Maria Press, 1982.
- Thomas, Leo, OP, and Jan Alkire. *Healing Ministry: A Practical Guide.* Kansas City: Sheed & Ward, 1994.
- Wuellner, Flora Slosson. *Release: Healing From Wounds of Family, Church, and Community.* Nashville: Upper Room, 1996.

ෆ *Alternative Forms of Healing*

- Dossey, Larry. *Healing Words: The Power of Prayer and the Practice of Medicine.* San Francisco: HarperSanFrancisco, 1993. (A little far-out in spots, but thought-provoking reading.)
- Krieger, Dolores. *Accepting Your Power to Heal: The Personal Practice of Therapeutic Touch.* Santa Fe, New Mexico: Bear & Co., 1993.

- Locke, Steven, M.D., and Douglass Colligan. *The Healer Within: The New Medicine of Mind and Body.* New American Library, 1986. (See especially Norman Cousins's introduction.)
- Macrae, Janet. *Therapeutic Touch: A Practical Guide.* New York: Knopf, 1987. (The best book from which to learn.)
- Wilkinson, William B. *The Bible and Healing: A Medical and Theological Commentary.* Grand Rapids, Michigan: Eerdmann's, 1998.

ᴄ︎ᴈ Exorcism and Deliverance

- Basham, Don. *Deliver Us From Evil.* Grand Rapids, Michigan: Chosen Books, 1972. (Well-written book by a Protestant clergyman, about his personal experience in learning about deliverance.)
- England, Dorothy Marie. *Satan Stalking.* Cincinnati: Forward Movement Publications, 1993.
- Linn, Matthew and Dennis Linn, eds. *Deliverance Prayer.* New York: Paulist, 1981. (An excellent introduction by two Jesuits long active in the healing ministry.)
- MacNutt, Francis. *Deliverance From Evil Spirits: A Practical Manual.* Grand Rapids, Michigan: Chosen Books, 1995.
- Richards, John. *But Deliver Us From Evil: An Introduction to the Demonic in Pastoral Care.* New York: Seabury, 1974. (By far the best book on the subject. Thorough, sane, scholarly, readable. Unfortunately, it is out of print.)
- Sandford, John Loren, and Mark Sandford. *Deliverance and Inner Healing.* Grand Rapids: Chosen Books, 1992.
- Wink, Walter. *Naming the Powers: The Language of Power in the New Testament.* Philadelphia: Fortress, 1984.

• ————. *Unmasking the Powers: The Invisible Forces That Determine Human Existence.* Philadelphia: Fortress, 1986.
• ————. *Engaging the Powers: Discernment and Resistance in a World of Domination.* Philadelphia: Fortress, 1992.

Resources for Healing Services

The following pages contain resources that we put together for use at Saint Luke's Episcopal Church in Darien, Connecticut. Morehouse Publishing has agreed to grant permission to photocopy these pages for use in church services, provided full copyright credit is given, and the pages have been typeset to fit an average church leaflet size. The resources provided here include a litany of healing, a service of healing that is incorporated into the Holy Eucharist, suggestions for hymns, and a service of commissioning for those called to the healing ministry.

The litany of healing was compiled by Saint Luke's Healing Ministries, Darien, from several sources, including the *Litany of Healing* by Morton Stone in *Prayer Book Studies #25,* published by Church Hymnal, and a litany used in the *Presiding Bishop's National Day of Prayer for Persons Living with HIV-AIDS.*

The service of healing is integrated into the Holy Eucharist, Rite Two of the *Book of Common Prayer* of the Episcopal Church. Additional prayers and instructions have been added by members of Saint Luke's Healing Ministries, Darien. An outline for the service leaflet is provided, and is followed by an Order of Service for the officiants.

The healing service with the Holy Eucharist is followed by suggestions for hymns that would be appropriate for a healing service. The hymns were chosen for their suitable words and ease of singing, and, although most are taken from the Episcopal *Hymnal 1982,* they can be found in the hymnals of other denominations.

Finally, a service of commitment to the healing ministry is provided for parishes who wish to commission their ministers of healing. The service was written for Saint Luke's by Anne Kimball and may easily be inserted before or after the Peace during a Sunday or weekday service of the Holy Eucharist in the Episcopal Church.

For the services from other denominations I would suggest the following sources:

Blessed to be a Blessing, by Methodist James K. Wagner, contains nine different healing services. Some include Holy Communion and some do not. Available from Upper Room Books, Box 189, 1908 Grand Avenue, Nashville, Tennessee 37202.

Roman Catholics have many provisions for healing prayer. The primary one is *The Sacrament of the Sick*, found in *The Rites of the Catholic Church* (New York: Pueblo Publishing, 1976), pp. 573-642.

The Presbyterians have a "Service for Wholeness" in *Services for Occasions of Pastoral Care*, available from John Knox/Westminster Press, 100 Witherspoon St., Louisville, Kentucky 40202-1396.

The United Church of Christ includes a healing service in their *Book of Worship: United Church of Christ*. Available from the Office of Church Life and Leadership in Cleveland, Ohio. Phone: 216-736-2130.

Healing services for Lutherans are available from the Division of Congregational Ministries, 8765 West Higgins Road, Chicago, Illinois 60631-4188.

♋ *A Litany of Healing*

Lord Jesus, you healed all who came to you in faith and sent forth your disciples to preach the Gospel and heal the sick;
We praise and thank you, O God.

God of grace, you nurture us with a love deeper than we know, and your will for us is healing and salvation;
We praise and thank you, O God.

God of love, you enter into our lives, our pain and our brokenness, and you stretch out your healing hands to us wherever we are;
We praise and thank you, O God.

Touch and heal our hearts burdened by anguish, despair and isolation, and set us free in love;
Hear us, and make us whole.

Give patience, courage, and faith to all who are disabled by injury or sickness;
Hear us, and make us whole.

Grant your strengthening presence to all who are about to undergo an operation;
Hear us, and make us whole.

As used in Saint Luke's Parish, Darien, Connecticut, and reprinted in *Healing in the Landscape of Prayer* by Avery Brooke (Cambridge, Mass.: Cowley Publications, 1996).

Sustain those who face long illness, bearing them up as on
eagles' wings;
Hear us and make us whole.

Comfort and relieve those who endure continual pain,
pouring upon them the sweet balm of your spirit;
Hear us and make us whole.

Grant to all sufferers the refreshment of quiet sleep;
Hear us and make us whole.

Give your wisdom in ample measure to doctors and nurses,
that with knowledge, skill, and patience they may minister to the sick;
Hear us and make us whole.

Guide all who search for the causes of sickness and disease;
Hear us and make us whole.

Break the bonds of our imprisonment to fear, compulsion,
and addiction;
Come with your healing power, O God.

Give us liberty from old hurts and painful memories;
Come with your healing power, O God.

Fill us with peace in our grief from separation and loss;
Come with your healing power, O God.

Work through all who share in your ministry of healing,
and renew us in compassion and strength;
Come with your healing power, O God.

God of strength, you fill us with your presence and send us
forth in love and healing among those we meet;
We praise and thank you, O God.

Touch and heal our bodies suffering from sickness, injury,
and disability, and make us whole again;
Hear us and make us whole.

Touch and heal our minds from darkness, confusion, and
doubt, and fill them with your light;
Come with your healing power, O God.

Let us pray.

O God, in you all darkness is turned to light and all
brokenness is make whole: Look with compassion on
us and those for whom we pray, that we may be re-
created in our Savior Jesus Christ. *Amen.*

You may add your own intercessions and thanksgivings,
either silently or aloud.

ᘓ Holy Eucharist and Healing Service
Service Leaflet

Hymn

The Holy Eucharist   BCP, p. 355

The Collect

First Reading

Psalm

Gospel

Meditation or Homily

Litany of Healing   Bulletin insert

Confession   BCP, p. 360

Hymn *(sung kneeling)*

Anointing and Laying on of Hands

> *Please wait for the ushers to direct those who wish to go forward for the laying on of hands. Go first to the priest, who will anoint you, then to whichever minister of healing is free. If you have a special request, you may make it known to the ministers of healing before they pray with you. If you need assistance or prefer the ministers to come to you, please inform an usher.*

As used in Saint Luke's Parish, Darien, Connecticut, and reprinted in *Healing in the Landscape of Prayer* by Avery Brooke (Cambridge, Mass.: Cowley Publications, 1996).

During the laying on of hands, before and after you go for-ward, we ask your prayers for those currently at the altar rail.

The Peace

The Offertory

The Great Thanksgiving

All are welcome to receive communion.
The invitation is the Lord's.

Closing Prayer *(said in unison)*:

Almighty and eternal God, so draw our hearts to you, so guide our minds, so fill our imaginations, so control our wills, that we may be wholly yours, ut-terly dedicated to you; and then use us, we pray, as you will, and always to your glory and the welfare of your people; through our Lord and Savior Jesus Christ. Amen.

Benediction

Hymn

Dismissal

␃ *Holy Eucharist and Healing Service*
Order of Service for Officiants

Hymn: Announce the number twice from the back of the chapel and then the Celebrant and assistants process in.

Welcome

The Holy Eucharist: Book of Common Prayer, p. 355

Collect: In place of the Collect of the Day, the Celebrant may say one of the following:

> O God of peace, you have taught us that in returning and rest we shall be saved, in quietness and in confidence shall be our strength: By the might of your Spirit lift us, we pray, to your presence, where we may be still and know that you are God; through Jesus Christ our Lord, who lives and reigns with you and the Holy Spirit, one God, for ever and ever. *Amen.*

> *or*

> Almighty God, who inspired your servant Luke the physician to set forth in the Gospel the love and healing power of your Son: Graciously continue in your Church this love and power to heal, to the praise and glory of your Name; through Jesus Christ

---

As used in Saint Luke's Parish, Darien, Connecticut, and reprinted in *Healing in the Landscape of Prayer* by Avery Brooke (Cambridge, Mass.: Cowley Publications, 1996).

our Lord, who lives and reigns with you, in the unity of the Holy Spirit, one God, now and for ever. *Amen.*

First Reading: Read by an appointed lay person.

Psalm: Led by an appointed lay person.

Gospel: Read by the Deacon or Celebrant.

Meditation or Homily: The homily at a healing service should be meditative in nature and may be as simple as pointing out one or two aspects of the lessons and then saying, "Let us meditate in silence upon the meaning of the lessons." The period of silence should be at least three or four minutes long, and can be brought to a close with the following prayer introducing the litany:

Most merciful God, we bring before your healing presence all those whom we carry on our hearts and in our prayers. You know all their needs. Grant that they too may have the consciousness of your presence, that their hearts too may be open to receive you. Bless them and heal them. Use us and our prayers as it may please you, in this your service. We ask this through your Son, Jesus Christ. *Amen.*

Litany of Healing: Led by an appointed lay person and introduced with the following words:

Our prayers now continue with a Litany of Healing.

Confession: Book of Common Prayer, page 360.

Hymn: Announce the next hymn, which should be sung kneeling. During the first verse the lay ministers will come

forward for anointing and to pray for each other. When
the hymn has been sung and the lay ministers have been
anointed and prayed for, the following invitation is given:

And now those who are in any way troubled or dis-
tressed by the things of this world, those who desire
help and strength in overcoming pain or illness in
body, mind, or spirit, for themselves or for others,
come forward and receive the laying on of hands
with faith.

Laying on of Hands and Anointing: People come forward as
guided by an usher. The Celebrant stands in the center, a
few steps forward of the altar rail, and anoints people with
blessed oil before they go to the stations, where one or two
members of the healing team will lay on hands. When all
have had their turn, the Celebrant and any assistants may
come forward for prayers if desired.

The laying on of hands may be concluded with the following prayers:

We thank you, God, for the healing that you have
accomplished and begun in us. *Amen.*

Then say one of the following:

Bless us, O God, with a sense of your presence and
companionship, that in the strength of it we may
walk as children of light. Open wide the windows of
your spirits, and fill us with light; open wide the
doors of our hearts that we may receive and welcome
you as the Guest and Master of our lives. Take our
lips and speak through them; take our minds and
kindle them with thought of you; take our hearts
and wills and set them on fire to do your will, and to

serve your children. All this we ask in the name of your Son and our Savior, Jesus Christ. *Amen.*

or

Almighty God, you are the only source of health and healing, the spirit of calm, and the central peace of the universe. We ask that you would fill us with such an awareness of your presence within that we may have complete confidence in you. In all pain and weariness and anxiety may we rest in your protecting care; may we know ourselves to be encircled by your loving power so that we may allow you to give us health and strength and peace, through Jesus Christ, our Lord. *Amen.*

The Peace

Offertory Sentences

The Great Thanksgiving

Closing Prayer: In place of or in addition to the usual post-communion prayer, the congregation may join in the following prayer, as printed in the service leaflet.

Almighty and eternal God, so draw our hearts to you, so guide our minds, so fill our imaginations, so control our wills, that we may be wholly yours, utterly dedicated to you; and then use us, we pray, as you will, and always to your glory and the welfare of your people; through our Lord and Savior Jesus Christ. *Amen.*

Benediction: The following blessing may be used.

The peace of God, which passes all understanding, keep your hearts and minds in the knowledge and love of God, and of his Son Jesus Christ, our Lord; and the blessing of God Almighty, the Father, the Son, and the Holy Spirit, rest upon you and those for whom you have prayed, now and always. *Amen.*

Hymn: Announce the number of the closing hymn and process out. The lay assistant or acolyte should extinguish the candles during the hymn.

Dismissal: The Deacon or Celebrant says one of the following sentences:

Go forth into the world, rejoicing in the power of the Spirit.
Thanks be to God

or

Let us go forth in the name of Christ.
Thanks be to God.

∞ *Appropriate Hymns for a Healing Service*

Opening
Come, thou long-expected Jesus
Brightest and best of the stars of the morning
Come, thou almighty King
O love, how deep, how broad, how high (verses 1-3)
Alleluia! sing to Jesus! (not during Lent)
Come, my Way, my Truth, my Life
Breathe on me, Breath of God
Come, Holy Spirit, heavenly Dove
Like the murmur of the dove's song
Come down, O Love divine
The King of love my shepherd is (verses 1-3)
Love divine, all loves excelling
O for a closer walk with God
Just as I am, without one plea
Seek ye first the kingdom of God

Middle
Spirit of the Living God
Fairest Lord Jesus
Praise, my soul, the King of heaven
Immortal, invisible, God only wise
In the cross of Christ I glory
There's a wideness in God's mercy
Lord of all hopefulness, Lord of all joy
I want to walk as a child of the light
Lead us, heavenly Father, lead us
Father eternal, Ruler of creation
Jesu, Jesu, fill us with your love

Middle, continued
Dear Lord and Father of mankind
O Master, let me walk with thee
Take my life, and let it be
Amazing grace! how sweet the sound
There is a balm in Gilead

Closing
Now the day is over
As with gladness men of old
Jesus is Lord
Come, thou almighty King
Thou, whose almighty word
Joyful, joyful, we adore thee
Praise to the Lord, the Almighty
Now thank we all our God
In the cross of Christ I glory
Awake, my soul, stretch every nerve
Fight the good fight with all thy might
How firm a foundation, ye saints of the Lord

⌘ A Service of Commitment to Healing Ministry

Celebrant: Will those making a commitment to the study and the practice of the ministry of healing please come forward.

Throughout church history, healing ministries have brought hope and comfort to those who turn to Jesus Christ in faith. You now come to commit yourselves to this ministry, as you offer yourselves in service in his name.

Have you undertaken at least a year of study and prayer for the special ministry of healing?

Healing Ministers: I have done so, to the best of my ability.

Celebrant: Do you intend to participate in this ministry reverently, and in accordance with the teaching Jesus Christ?

Healing Ministers: I do, with God's help.

Celebrant: Do you commit yourself, before God, to reach out with love and compassion to those who are sick in body, mind, or spirit?

Healing Ministers: I do, with God's help.

Written for Saint Luke's Parish, Darien, Connecticut, by Anne Kimball. Reprinted from *Healing in the Landscape of Prayer* by Avery Brooke (Cambridge, Mass.: Cowley Publications, 1996).

Celebrant: Will you strive to serve in the name of Christ, acknowledging that it is his spirit that heals and his love that binds us together?

Healing Ministers: I will, with God's help.

Celebrant: Will you seek to grow in your understanding of God's will in all you do, devoting yourselves to a regular time of prayer, study, and practice?

Healing Ministers: I will, with God's help.

Celebrant: In the name of this congregation, I commend you to this work, and pledge to you our prayers, encouragement, and support.

Let us pray.

Almighty God, look with favor upon these persons who come to you seeking your blessing. Enable them to minister with humility your healing power, that they may reach out with faith and confidence. Fill them with your holy and life-giving Spirit, that they may be empowered to do your work in the world according to your will. All this we ask in the name of your Son Jesus Christ, who came to serve and brought your healing power into the world. *Amen.*